SUPER EASY

Soups AND Stews

SUPER EASY Soups AND Stews

100 Soups, Stews, Broths, Chilis, Chowders, and More!

EDITED BY

ABIGAIL R. GEHRING

Good  Books®

New York, New York

Good Books books may be purchased in bulk at special discounts for sales promotion, corporate gifts, fund-raising, or educational purposes. Special editions can also be created to specifications. For details, contact the Special Sales Department, Good Books, 307 West 36th Street, 11th Floor, New York, NY 10018 or info@skyhorsepublishing.com.

Good Books is an imprint of Skyhorse Publishing, Inc.®, a Delaware corporation.

Visit our website at www.goodbooks.com.

10 9 8 7 6 5 4 3 2

Library of Congress Cataloging-in-Publication Data is available on file.

Cover design by Brian Peterson
Cover photo courtesy of Getty Images

Print ISBN: 978-1-68099-482-7
Ebook ISBN: 978-1-68099-483-4

Printed in China

Contents

Introduction

There's nothing quite like a nourishing bowl of chicken soup when you're under the weather, a pot of chili for the big game, or a good seafood chowder on a summer evening at the beach house. In fact, I'd argue that there's a soup, stew, chili, or chowder for every occasion. Soups are so versatile—they're the little black dress of the culinary world. Dress them up for a fancy event, dress them down for lunch at the office. And perhaps best of all, many are so easy to make!

What makes these soups "Super Easy?" The recipes in this book—collected from some of the smartest home cooks across the country—all require 30 minutes or less of preparation time. For days when even half an hour is too much, the recipes marked with a "Quick Prep" icon in the top corner of the page all require 15 minutes or less of prep work. Once the ingredients are in the pot, most recipes allow you to leave the soup simmering while you go take care of other matters (or just relax!). Some may ask for a quick stir now and again or a final step of adding an ingredient or blending everything together for a smooth, creamy soup. If you'll need to leave the house while the soup is simmering, opt for one of the recipes with the slow cooker icon on top—cooking in a slow cooker (or with the slow cooker setting on your multi-cooker) takes longer, but you're free to go to sleep or leave the house without worrying about an open flame.

Choosing a Pot

There's no rule saying you have to cook your soup in any particular kind of pot, but a pot with some substance will help prevent burning on the bottom when cooking thicker soups and stews. Technically, a stock pot has a flat base, tall sides, and a lid, and is often made of thin aluminum, stainless steel, or heat-resistant glass. Stock pots are fine for making stocks, broths, or other thin soups. But if you're investing in one new pot, I'd go with a soup pot or Dutch oven, both of which are made of heavier materials—often cast iron with a colorful enamel coating. Not only are they more versatile for soup-making, but they'll come in handy for a variety of other cooking purposes—soup pots are perfect for making pasta, for example, and Dutch ovens bake a great loaf of sourdough.

Slow cookers are also a great help to busy home cooks since, as mentioned earlier, you can leave them to do their job without worrying about an open flame in your home. They do require longer cook times, so when you see the slow cooker icon above a recipe, know you'll need to plan ahead several hours. If you don't have a slow cooker but intend to get one, consider opting for a multi-cooker (such as an Instant Pot) to get more bang for your buck. Multi-cookers can operate as pressure cookers as well, and some can even sauté, bake, steam, fry, and more.

Stocking Your Pantry and Freezer

There are a handful of ingredients you'll see over and over again in these recipes, so you may as well stock up next time you see a good sale.

Pantry:
Chicken stock and/or broth
Beef stock and/or broth
Vegetable stock and/or broth
Black beans
Kidney beans
Pinto beans
Canned corn
Canned diced tomatoes

Freezer:
Boneless, skinless chicken breasts
Ground beef
Frozen veggies (corn, peas, carrots, mixed)

Spice Shelf:
Bay leaves
Chili powder
Cumin
Garlic cloves
Oregano
Salt and pepper
Thyme

Stocks vs. Broths

Stock and broth are interchangeable in most recipes, so if you see one called for and only have the other, feel free to use what you have. Stock is usually made from simmering the meat bones for long periods, which results in more gelatin in the liquid. This adds a richer texture and more nutrients than broth has, which is made with more meat than bones. To make your own meat stocks or vegetable broth, see pages 2–4.

Freezing Your Soups, Stews, Chilis, and Chowders

One of the best parts of making a big pot of soup is being able to freeze some for another day, or to gift to a loved one when they're ill, just had a baby, or could just use a quick meal! Allow your soup to cool and then ladle into plastic containers with tight lids, glass canning jars, or re-sealable plastic bags. Whatever you use, be sure to leave extra space, as liquids expand as they freeze. This is especially important if you're using glass jars—you don't want glass shattering all over your freezer! Label your container with the kind of soup and the date. Most soups will stay good for at least four months in the freezer, often much longer.

To thaw, place the container in a bowl of warm water until the soup becomes more like a slushy (big chunks are fine). Then pour into a pot and simmer until hot.

Pro Tips

- Keeping soups and stews at a simmer allows all the ingredients to cook through evenly. Be careful not to boil too vigorously—you'll end up with tough meat and possibly a very messy stove.
- Taking the time to sauté your onions and garlic in a bit of butter or olive oil prior to adding your liquids will create a much richer layer of flavor in your soup.
- Soups are great for utilizing food scraps (toss that Parmesan cheese rind in your broth!) and less "pretty" vegetables (that gnarled carrot in the veggie drawer, those weirdly shaped potatoes). Veggie scraps (onion skins, celery tops) can also be used to make great stocks and broths.
- Chopping veggies does take time. Good quality, sharp knives will make the job faster and safer. Hold the knife between your thumb and pointer finger at the base of the blade and allow the other fingers to wrap around the top of the handle for the most control. Don't grip too tightly—you want a secure grasp, but not a rigid one. You can also prep veggies ahead of time and keep them in re-sealable plastic bags for a day or two prior to making your soup.
- Immersion blenders (or "stick blenders") are great for making creamy soups. It's much easier to put an immersion blender in the pot and hit the on switch than to transfer everything from your soup pot to a blender or food processor.
- To thicken a soup quickly near the end of your cooking time, make a slurry by whisking together equal parts cornstarch and cold water (start with a few tablespoons of each for a medium-sized pot of soup). Add to soup slowly, stir or whisk, and simmer to thicken. If it's still not thick enough after a few minutes, you can repeat. Note that you need the heat of a simmer or slow boil in order to activate the starch—don't try adding your slurry to a cold soup or stew and expect it to work without heating.

Customizing Recipes

Most soup recipes are pretty flexible, meaning you can customize them to your own dietary needs, preferences, and what you have on hand. Just keep in mind that larger or denser veggies take longer to cook, so, for example, chunks of butternut squash may be added early in a soup's cook time, whereas frozen peas or kale should be tossed in a few minutes before the soup is done to avoid winding up with mush. Vegetable broth can certainly be used in place of any meat broth or stock, and gluten-free noodles can replace regular pasta. Ground turkey can be used in place of ground beef for a leaner option. Herbs and spices can be adjusted to taste. Most pages have a bit of blank space available where you can make your own notes as desired.

Stocks, Broths & Soups

Chicken Stock

**Shari Jensen,
Fountain, CO**

Makes 12 servings
Prep. Time: 5 minutes
Cooking Time: 8–10 hours
Ideal slow-cooker size: 5 qt.

1 carcass from roasted chicken or turkey, or about
   2 lbs. chicken backs, necks, wing tips, etc., fresh
   or left over from dinners

3 quarts water

½ cup dry white wine

3 medium carrots, chopped in large chunks

2 medium onions, cut in quarters

3 ribs celery with leaves on, chopped in large
   chunks

2 tsp. salt

3 whole cloves

1 bay leaf

1 tsp. dried thyme

5 peppercorns

1 Tbsp. dried parsley

2 large sage leaves, *optional*

2 cloves garlic, peeled, *optional*

1. Place chicken, water, wine, carrots, onions, celery, and salt in slow cooker or large stock pot.

2. Tie cloves, bay leaf, thyme, sage leaves, garlic, peppercorns, and parsley in a square of cheesecloth. Place in crock or pot.

3. Simmer on Low 8–10 hours in a slow cooker or at least 2–3 hours in a pot on the stovetop.

4. Cool. Remove cheesecloth packet. Strain Stock into a large bowl.

5. Cover and chill overnight. If desired, skim solidified fat off before using stock.

SLOW COOKER

QUICK PREP

Beef Stock

**Margaret W. High,
Lancaster, PA**

Makes 20 servings
Prep. Time: 10 minutes
Cooking Time: 12–24 hours
Ideal slow-cooker size: 6 qt.

3 lbs. meaty beef bones, preferably with marrow

1 onion, unpeeled, cut in chunks

1 tsp. salt

5 peppercorns

1 Tbsp. vinegar

water

1. Place all ingredients in crock, adding water to within 1" of top, or in a large stock pot and add water to cover all ingredients.

2. Cover and simmer on Low for 12–24 hours in the slow cooker or 2–3 hours in a pot on the stovetop, or however much time you have, adding more water as needed.

3. Allow Stock to cool for an hour or two before straining. Be sure to get the marrow out into the strainer and press on everything to get all the good stuff into the stock.

4. If desired, de-fat the stock by chilling it and lifting off the layer of solidified fat or by using a fat separator with the warm stock.

5. Keep stock in fridge for up to a week, or freeze in containers.

SLOW COOKER

Vegetable Broth

Rebekah Zehr,
Lowville, NY

Makes 6–8 servings
Prep. Time: 5 minutes
Cooking Time: 6 hours
Ideal slow-cooker size: 3 qt.

4 cups vegetable scraps

2–3 sprigs herbs such as
 rosemary and thyme

2–3 cloves garlic

1" piece ginger, *optional*

8 cups water

1. Combine ingredients in slow cooker or large stock pot. Water should just cover everything.

2. Cover and simmer on Low for 6 hours in a slow cooker or about an hour in a pot on the stovetop.

3. Strain broth, pressing on vegetables in strainer to get all the good stuff.

4. Store broth in canning jars in fridge for up to 2 weeks, or freeze.

TIP

Onions, carrots, and celery are basics for broth, but feel free to add any veggies or fresh herbs that you have on hand. Don't bother peeling them or trimming away stalks.

SLOW COOKER

Chicken Wild Rice Soup

Joyce Shackelford,
Green Bay, WI

Makes 8 servings
Prep. Time: 25 minutes
Cooking Time: 3–4 hours
Ideal slow-cooker size: 4-qt.

2 Tbsp. butter

½ cup dry wild rice

6 cups chicken stock

½ cup minced onions

½ cup minced celery

½ lb. winter squash, peeled, seeded, cut in
    ½" cubes

2 cups chicken, chopped and cooked

½ cup browned, slivered almonds

1. Melt butter in small skillet. Add rice and sauté 10 minutes over low heat. Transfer to slow cooker.

2. Add all remaining ingredients except chicken and almonds.

3. Cover. Cook on Low 3–4 hours, or until vegetables are cooked to your liking. One hour before serving, stir in chicken.

4. Top with browned slivered almonds just before serving.

Chicken Spinach Soup

**Carna Reitz,
Remington, VA**

Makes 4–6 servings
Prep. Time: 5 minutes
Cooking Time: 20 minutes

6½ cups chicken broth, *divided*

2 cups cooked chicken

1–2 cups frozen chopped spinach

salt and pepper, to taste

½ cup flour

1. Put 6 cups broth, chicken, spinach, and salt and pepper in a large stockpot. Bring to a boil.

2. Meanwhile, mix flour and remaining ½ cup broth together in a jar. Put on lid and shake until smooth. When soup is boiling, slowly pour into soup to thicken, stirring constantly.

3. Continue stirring and cooking until soup thickens.

Chicken Barley Soup

**Ida H. Goering,
Dayton, VA**

Makes 6 servings
Prep. Time: 20 minutes
Cooking Time: 1 hour

6 cups chicken broth

1½ cups diced carrots

1 cup diced celery

½ cup chopped onion

¼ cup uncooked barley

2–3 cups (about 6 oz.) cooked and cut-up chicken

14½-oz. can diced tomatoes, no salt added, undrained

½ tsp. black pepper

1 bay leaf

2 Tbsp. chopped fresh parsley, or 2 tsp. dried parsley

1. Combine all ingredients except parsley in large kettle.

2. Cover and bring to boil.

3. Simmer, covered, for one hour. Stir occasionally.

4. Just before serving, remove bay leaf. Stir in parsley.

Chicken Tortellini Soup

**Mary Seielstad,
Sparks, NV**

Makes 4–6 servings
Prep. Time: 10–15 minutes
Cooking Time: 25 minutes

1 Tbsp. butter

4 cloves garlic, minced

5 cups chicken broth

9-oz. pkg. frozen cheese tortellini

1½ cups diced cooked chicken

14-oz. can stewed tomatoes

10-oz. pkg. frozen spinach

½ tsp. pepper

1 tsp. dried basil

¼ cup grated Parmesan cheese

1. In large saucepan, melt butter and sauté garlic for 2 minutes over medium heat.

2. Stir in broth and tortellini and bring to a boil. Cover, reduce heat, and simmer 5 minutes.

3. Add cooked chicken, tomatoes, frozen spinach, pepper, and basil and simmer 10–15 minutes. Stir every 3 minutes or so, breaking up frozen spinach and blending it into the soup.

4. Serve when soup is heated through, along with Parmesan cheese to spoon over individual servings.

TIP

If you plan to freeze any soup with pasta in it, you can hold off on adding the pasta until you're re-heating the soup. It's not necessary, but the pasta will taste a little fresher that way.

Chicken Taco Soup

**Mary Puskar,
Forest Hill, MD**

Makes 4 servings
Prep. Time: 25 minutes
Cooking Time: 40 minutes

2 chicken breast halves

3 cups water

2 stalks celery

1 medium-sized onion

2 carrots

2 Tbsp. vegetable or canola oil

1 Tbsp. chili powder

1 Tbsp. cumin

4½-oz. can green chilies

14-oz. can chicken broth

14-oz. can beef broth

14½-oz. can diced tomatoes, undrained

1 Tbsp. Worcestershire sauce

tortilla chips, broken

Monterey Jack cheese, grated

1. In a large stockpot, cook chicken breasts in water until tender. Remove meat, reserving cooking water. When chicken is cool enough to handle, chop into bite-sized pieces. Set aside.

2. Chop celery and onion. Grate carrots.

3. In stockpot used for cooking chicken, sauté vegetables in oil.

4. Combine all ingredients in stockpot, except the cooked chicken, tortilla chips, and cheese. Cover and simmer 15 minutes.

5. Add diced chicken. Heat through.

6. Top each serving with broken tortilla chips and grated cheese.

Roasted Chicken Noodle Soup

Janie Steele,
Moore, OK

Makes 8 servings
Prep. Time: 30 minutes
Cooking Time: 5½–6½ hours
Ideal slow-cooker size: 5-qt.

1 cup chopped onions

1 cup chopped carrots

1 cup chopped celery

1 clove garlic, minced

2 tsp. olive or canola oil

1 tsp. flour

1½ tsp. fresh chopped oregano

1½ tsp. fresh chopped thyme

¼ tsp. poultry seasoning

6 cups chicken broth

4 cups diced potatoes

1 tsp. salt

2 cups skinless roasted chicken, diced

2 cups uncooked wide noodles

1 cup evaporated milk

1. Brown onions, carrots, celery, and garlic in oil in skillet.

2. Stir in flour, oregano, thyme, and poultry seasoning and blend well. Pour into slow cooker.

3. Mix in broth, potatoes, and salt.

4. Cook on Low 5–6 hours, or until potatoes are soft.

5. Add chicken, noodles, and milk. Cook until noodles are tender. Do not bring to a boil after milk is added.

Chicken and Vegetable Soup with Rice

Hope Comerford,
Clinton Township, MI

Makes 4–6 servings
Prep. Time: 20 minutes
Cooking Time: 6½–7½ hours
Ideal slow-cooker size: 3-qt.

1½–2 lbs. boneless, skinless chicken breasts

1½ cups chopped carrots

1½ cups chopped red onion

4 cloves garlic, chopped

1 Tbsp. onion powder

2 tsp. salt (you can omit the salt if you're using regular stock rather than no-salt)

¼ tsp. celery seed

¼ tsp. paprika

⅛ tsp. pepper

1 dried bay leaf

8 cups no-salt chicken stock

1 cup fresh green beans

3 cups cooked rice

1. Place chicken into the bottom of crock, then add rest of the remaining ingredients, except green beans and rice.

2. Cover and cook on Low for 6–7 hours.

3. Remove chicken and chop into bite-sized cubes. Place chicken back into crock and add in green beans. Cover and cook another 30 minutes. Remove bay leaf and discard.

4. To serve, place approximately ½ cup of the cooked rice into each bowl and ladle soup over top of the rice.

Bean Soup with Turkey Sausage

**Dorothy Reise,
Severna Park, MD
D. Fern Ruth,
Chalfont, PA**

Makes 4 servings
Prep. Time: 15–20 minutes
Cooking Time: 15–20 minutes

8 oz. turkey kielbasa

4 cups chicken broth

2 15-oz. cans cannelloni beans, drained and rinsed

½–1 cup onion, chopped

2 tsp. fresh minced basil

¼ tsp. coarsely ground pepper

1 clove garlic, minced

1 carrot, peeled and sliced, or 1 cup baby carrots

half a red, yellow, or orange bell pepper, sliced

3 cups fresh spinach, cleaned

¼ cup fresh chopped parsley

1. Cut turkey kielbasa lengthwise, and then into ½" slices. Sauté in Dutch oven or large saucepan until browned, stirring occasionally so it doesn't stick.

2. Combine all ingredients in pan except spinach and parsley.

3. Bring to boil, and then reduce heat. Cover and simmer 10–15 minutes, or until onion and carrots are tender.

4. If you're using frozen spinach, add it to the soup and let it thaw in the soup pot. Stir occasionally to break up spinach and to have it heat through.

5. If you're using fresh spinach, remove stems from fresh spinach, stack, and cut into 1" strips. Remove soup from heat and stir in spinach and parsley until spinach wilts.

6. Serve immediately.

Ground Turkey Soup

**Betty K. Drescher,
Quakertown, PA**

Makes 12 servings
Prep. Time: 20–30 minutes
Cooking Time: 8–9 hours
Ideal slow-cooker size: 5- or 6-qt.

1 lb. ground turkey

1 cup onions, chopped

1 clove garlic, minced

15-oz. can kidney beans, drained

1 cup sliced carrots

1 cup sliced celery

¼ cup long-grain rice, uncooked

1 qt. low-sodium diced Italian tomatoes

2 cups fresh green beans

2 tsp. fresh chopped parsley

half a green bell pepper, chopped

1 tsp. salt

⅛ tsp. black pepper

1 Tbsp. Worcestershire sauce

1 bay leaf

3 cups water

1. Brown turkey in a large nonstick skillet.

2. Combine with remaining ingredients in slow cooker.

3. Cover. Cook on Low 8–9 hours. Remove bay leaf and discard before serving.

Turkey Sausage and Cabbage Soup

**Bonita Stutzman,
Harrisonburg, VA**

Makes 8 servings
Prep. Time: 20 minutes
Cooking Time: 1 hour, or more

1½ cups chopped onions

2 cloves garlic, finely chopped

¾ lb. turkey sausage, chopped in small pieces

6 cups shredded green cabbage

3 lbs. canned tomatoes, no salt added, undrained

1½ qts. water

1 Tbsp. dried basil

2 tsp. dried oregano

¼ tsp. black pepper

1. Spray inside bottom of stockpot lightly with cooking spray. Sauté onions and garlic until tender.

2. Add chopped sausage. Cook until lightly browned.

3. Stir in remaining ingredients.

4. Cover. Simmer until cabbage is very tender, about an hour.

Turkey Rosemary Veggie Soup

Willard E. Roth, Elkhart, IN

Makes 8 servings
Prep. Time: 30 minutes
Cooking Time: 8 hours
Ideal slow-cooker size: 6-qt.

1 lb. ground turkey

3 parsley stalks with leaves, sliced

3 scallions, chopped

3 medium carrots, unpeeled, sliced

3 medium potatoes, unpeeled, sliced

3 celery ribs with leaves, sliced

3 small onions, sliced

2 cups whole-kernel corn

2 cups fresh green beans

16-oz. can low-sodium diced Italian-style tomatoes

3 cups vegetable broth

3 Tbsp. fresh chopped rosemary

1. Brown turkey with parsley and scallions in nonstick skillet. Drain. Pour into slow cooker sprayed with nonstick spray.

2. Add vegetables, tomatoes, vegetable broth, and rosemary.

3. Cover. Cook on Low 8 hours, or until vegetables are done to your liking.

Tuscany Peasant Soup

Alice Valine,
Elma, NY

Makes 8 servings
Prep. Time: 20 minutes
Cooking Time: 25 minutes

½ lb. bulk turkey sausage

1 onion, chopped

2–3 cloves garlic, minced

2 15-oz. cans cannellini beans, or great northern beans, rinsed and drained

2 14½-oz. cans diced tomatoes, no salt added, undrained

2 14-oz. cans chicken broth

2 tsp. no-salt Italian seasoning

3 medium zucchini, sliced

4 cups fresh spinach leaves, chopped, or baby spinach, unchopped

shredded Parmesan or Romano cheese, *optional*

1. In Dutch oven or stockpot, cook sausage over medium heat until no longer pink. Drain off drippings.

2. Add onion and garlic. Sauté until tender.

3. Stir in beans, tomatoes, broth, seasoning, and zucchini. Cook uncovered 10 minutes.

4. Add spinach and heat until just wilted.

5. Serve with cheese, if you wish.

Italian Sausage Soup

**Esther Porter,
Minneapolis, MN**

Makes 6-8 servings
Prep. Time: 15-25 minutes
Cooking Time: 65-70 minutes

1 lb. Italian sausage, casings removed

1 cup chopped onions

2 large cloves garlic, sliced

5 cups beef stock, or 3 14½-oz. cans beef broth

2 cups chopped or canned tomatoes

8-oz. can tomato sauce

1½ cups sliced zucchini

1 carrot, thinly sliced

1 medium-sized green bell pepper, diced

1 cup green beans, frozen or fresh

2 Tbsp. dried basil

2 Tbsp. dried oregano

8-10-oz. pkg. cheese tortellini

salt, to taste

pepper, to taste

freshly grated Parmesan cheese for topping

1. Sauté sausage in heavy Dutch oven over medium heat until cooked through, about 10 minutes, breaking it up with a wooden spoon as it browns.

2. Using a slotted spoon, transfer sausage to a large bowl. Pour off all but 1 Tbsp. drippings from Dutch oven. Add onions and garlic to the 1 Tbsp. drippings and sauté until clear, about 5 minutes.

3. Return sausage to pan. Add beef stock, tomatoes, tomato sauce, zucchini, carrot, pepper, green beans, basil, and oregano. Simmer 30–40 minutes, or until vegetables are tender.

4. Add tortellini and cook 8–10 minutes. Season to taste with salt and pepper.

5. Ladle hot soup into bowls and sprinkle with Parmesan cheese.

Broccoli Rabe and Sausage Soup

**Carlene Horne,
Bedford, NH**

Makes 4 servings
Prep. Time: 15 minutes
Cooking Time: 15 minutes

2 Tbsp. olive oil

1 onion, chopped

1 lb. sweet or spicy sausage, casing removed, sliced

1 bunch broccoli rabe, approximately 5 cups chopped

32 oz. chicken broth

1 cup water

8 oz. frozen tortellini

1. Heat olive oil in a soup pot.

2. Add onion and sausage and sauté until tender.

3. Add broccoli rabe and sauté a few more minutes.

4. Pour broth and water into pan; bring to simmer.

5. Add tortellini and cook a few minutes until tender.

TIPS

1. Substitute any green such as Swiss chard, kale, or spinach for the broccoli rabe.
2. Serve with grated cheese and crusty bread.

Meatball Tortellini Soup

Lucille Amos,
Greensboro, NC

Makes 4 servings
Prep. Time: 5 minutes
Cooking Time: 20–25 minutes

14-oz. can beef broth

12 frozen Italian meatballs

1 cup stewed tomatoes

11-oz. can Mexican-style corn, drained

1 cup (20) frozen cheese tortellini

1. Bring broth to boil in a large stockpot.

2. Add meatballs. Cover and reduce heat. Simmer 5 minutes.

3. Add tomatoes and corn. Cover and simmer 5 minutes more.

4. Add tortellini. Cover and simmer 5 more minutes, or until tortellini is tender.

Hearty Beef Barley Soup

Karen Gingrich,
New Holland, PA

Makes 4–5 servings
Preparation Time: 5–10 minutes
Cooking Time: 35 minutes

1 lb. beef tips

2 cups sliced fresh mushrooms

¼ tsp. garlic powder

32-oz. can (3½ cups) beef broth

2 medium-sized carrots, sliced

¼ tsp. dried thyme

dash of pepper

½ cup quick-cooking barley

1. Cook beef in nonstick saucepan until browned and juices evaporate, about 10 minutes, stirring often.

2. Add mushrooms and garlic powder and cook until mushrooms begin to wilt, about 5 minutes.

3. Add broth, carrots, thyme, and pepper.

4. Heat to boiling. Stir in barley. Cover and cook over low heat for 20 minutes, or until barley is tender.

Beef Minestrone Soup

**Lydia Konrad,
Edmonton, Alberta**

Makes 8–10 servings
Prep. Time: 15 minutes
Cooking Time: about 2 hours

1½ lbs. ground beef

1 cup diced onions

1 cup diced zucchini

1 cup cubed potatoes

1 cup sliced carrots

½ cup diced celery

1 cup shredded cabbage

15-oz. can tomatoes, chopped

1½ qts. water

1 bay leaf

½ tsp. dried thyme

2 tsp. salt

pepper, to taste

1 tsp. Worcestershire sauce

¼ cup uncooked brown rice

½ cup freshly grated Parmesan cheese

1. Brown ground beef in large soup kettle. Drain off grease.

2. Add vegetables, water, seasonings, and Worcestershire sauce and bring to a boil.

3. Sprinkle rice into mixture. Cover and simmer for at least 1 hour.

4. Remove bay leaf. Sprinkle with Parmesan cheese and serve with brown bread.

Creamy Ham and Veggie Soup

Chrissy Baldwin,
Mechanicsburg, PA

Makes 8–10 servings
Prep. Time: 20 minutes
Cooking Time: 35 minutes

3 cups diced potatoes

16-oz. frozen broccoli and cauliflower

1 cup chopped carrots

1 cup chopped onions

3 celery ribs, chopped

12-oz. ham cubes

4 chicken bouillon cubes

3 cups water

1 tsp. salt

¼ tsp. pepper

1 stick (8 Tbsp.) butter

½ cup flour

2 cups milk

1 cup shredded cheese

1. In soup pot, combine potatoes, broccoli and cauliflower, carrots, onions, celery, ham, bouillon, water, salt, and pepper. Simmer for 20 minutes or until vegetables are tender.

2. In separate saucepan, make a white sauce. Melt butter over low heat and stir in flour to make a thick paste. Whisk in milk. Bring to a boil and stir for 2–3 minutes.

3. Add white sauce to soup pot and simmer for 10 minutes.

4. Add shredded cheese and stir until melted.

Ham and Bean Soup

**Diane Eby,
Holtwood, PA**

Makes 6-8 servings
Prep. Time: 5 minutes
Cooking Time: 15-20 minutes

1 qt. water

2 cups fully cooked ham, diced

40½-oz. can great northern beans

½ lb. Velveeta cheese, cubed

1. Place water and ham in a large stockpot. Cook for 5 minutes.

2. Add beans. Heat through.

3. Add cheese. Stir until cheese melts.

Fresh Vegetable Soup

**Sandra Chang,
Derwood, MD**

Makes 4-6 servings
Prep. Time: 25-30 minutes
Cooking Time: 60-70 minutes
Standing Time: 1 hour

4 Tbsp. butter

½ cup of each:

  diced celery

  diced onions

  peeled carrots

  chopped cabbage

  diced zucchini

  fresh or frozen whole kernel corn

  fresh or frozen cut-up green beans

2 cups canned whole tomatoes

4 cups beef stock

2 Tbsp. sugar

salt, to taste

pepper, to taste

½ cup fresh or frozen petite peas

1. In 4-qt. saucepan, melt butter. Sauté celery, onions, carrots, cabbage, and zucchini in butter until vegetables are soft but not brown.

2. Add rest of ingredients, except ½ cup peas.

3. Simmer gently for 30–45 minutes, or until vegetables are cooked but not mushy.

4. Take pan off heat and stir in peas. Allow soup to stand for 1 hour before serving.

5. Reheat just until heated through and serve.

Wild Rice Mushroom Soup

**Kelly Amos,
Pittsboro, NC**

Makes 4 servings
Prep. Time: 15–20 minutes
Cooking Time: 35 minutes

1 Tbsp. olive oil

half a white onion, chopped

¼ cup chopped celery

¼ cup chopped carrots

1½ cups sliced fresh white mushrooms

½ cup white wine, or ½ cup chicken broth

2½ cups chicken broth

1 cup half-and-half

2 Tbsp. flour

¼ tsp. dried thyme

black pepper, to taste

1 cup cooked wild rice

1. Put olive oil in stockpot and heat. Carefully add chopped onion, celery, and carrots. Cook until tender.

2. Add mushrooms, white wine, and chicken broth.

3. Cover and heat through.

4. In a bowl, blend half-and-half, flour, thyme, and pepper. Then stir in cooked wild rice.

5. Pour rice mixture into hot stockpot with vegetables.

6. Cook over medium heat. Stir continually until thickened and bubbly.

Easy Cream of Vegetable Soup

**Norma Grieser,
Sebring, FL**

Makes 6 cups
Prep. Time: 20 minutes
Cooking Time: 20 minutes

¼ cup chopped celery

¼ cup chopped onion

1 Tbsp. canola oil

3 Tbsp. flour

½ tsp. salt

pepper, to taste

1 bay leaf, or herb of your choice

3 cups skim milk

2 cups fresh or frozen vegetables of your choice, cut up or sliced (spinach, asparagus, broccoli, cauliflower, peas, carrots, tomatoes, mushrooms); if using canned vegetables, use ones without added salt

1. In large stockpot, sauté celery and onion in oil.

2. Over low heat, stir in flour, salt, pepper, and herb.

3. Add milk, stirring constantly. Cook over medium heat until hot and bubbly.

4. Steam or microwave vegetables until crisp-tender.

5. Remove bay leaf, if using. Stir vegetables into thickened creamy sauce and heat through.

TIPS

1. If you want cream of chicken soup, add reduced-sodium chicken bouillon.
2. This recipe can be used as soup itself, or you can use it in any recipe calling for cream soup.

Apple Butternut Squash Soup

Ann Bender,
New Hope, VA

Makes 6 servings
Prep. Time: 30 minutes
Cooking Time: 30 minutes

3 cups butternut or acorn squash, peeled, seeded, and cubed

1 large apple, peeled and sliced

1½ Tbsp. chopped onion

1 clove garlic, minced

1 Tbsp. butter

2 Tbsp. flour

¾ tsp. fresh minced thyme

¼ tsp. salt

⅛ tsp. pepper

10½-oz. can chicken or vegetable broth

2 Tbsp. sour cream

1. Steam squash and apple in steamer or microwave until very tender.

2. In large saucepan, sauté onion and garlic in butter until onion is clear.

3. Stir flour and seasonings into saucepan.

4. Add broth. Heat, stirring continually until smooth and slightly thickened.

5. Pour broth and cooked vegetables into blender. Cover and blend carefully until smooth.

6. Serve immediately. Top each individual serving with 1 tsp. sour cream.

Veggie Minestrone

**Dorothy VanDeest,
Memphis, TN**

Makes 8 servings
Prep. Time: 15 minutes
Cooking Time: 25-30 minutes
Standing Time: 5-10 minutes

1 large onion, chopped

1 clove garlic, minced

4 cups chicken or vegetable broth

16-oz. can kidney beans, rinsed and drained

½ cup elbow macaroni, uncooked

14½-oz. can diced tomatoes, undrained, no salt added, or 5-6 whole tomatoes, peeled and chopped

2 medium carrots, sliced thin

¾ tsp. fresh chopped oregano

1 lb. fresh spinach, chopped

½ cup grated Parmesan cheese

1. Lightly spray or grease inside bottom of stockpot. Sauté onion and garlic until tender.

2. Add broth, beans, macaroni, tomatoes, carrots, and oregano.

3. Cover and cook until vegetables and macaroni are tender, about 20 minutes.

4. Stir in spinach. Bring to a boil.

5. Remove pan from heat. Let stand, covered, 5–10 minutes before serving.

6. Sprinkle 1 Tbsp. grated Parmesan on each individual bowl.

Pasta Fagioli

**Stacie Skelly,
Millersville, PA**

Makes 8–10 servings
Prep. Time: 20 minutes
Cooking Time: 1½ hours

1 lb. ground beef

1 cup diced onions

1 cup julienned carrots

1 cup chopped celery

2 cloves garlic, minced

2 14½-oz. cans diced tomatoes, undrained

15-oz. can red kidney beans, undrained

15-oz. can great northern beans, undrained

15-oz. can tomato sauce

12-oz. can V8 juice

1 Tbsp. vinegar

1½ tsp. salt

1 tsp. dried oregano

1 tsp. dried basil

½ tsp. pepper

½ tsp. dried thyme

½ lb. ditali pasta

1. Brown ground beef in a large stockpot. Drain off drippings.

2. To browned beef, add onions, carrots, celery, and garlic. Sauté for 10 minutes.

3. Add remaining ingredients, except pasta, and stir well. Simmer, covered, for 1 hour.

4. About 50 minutes into cooking time, cook pasta in a separate saucepan, according to the directions on the package.

5. Add drained pasta to the large pot of soup. Simmer for 5–10 minutes and serve.

TIP

If you can't find ditali pasta, you can substitute elbow macaroni.

Roasted Vegetable Gazpacho

**J. B. Miller,
Indianapolis, IN**

Makes 6 servings
Prep. Time: 30 minutes
Baking Time: 20–25 minutes
Chilling Time: 4 hours

2 red bell peppers, left whole

2 yellow bell peppers, left whole

2 large red onions, quartered

2 Tbsp. extra-virgin olive oil

black pepper, to taste

1 lb. (about 4 cups) medium zucchini, cut in
 ½-inch-thick slices

2 lbs. (about 7 medium) vine-ripened tomatoes,
 cored, quartered, and seeds removed

3 cloves garlic

2 Tbsp. chopped fresh basil

1 Tbsp. chopped fresh oregano

1 cup cold water

2 Tbsp. lime juice, or more to taste

1. Preheat oven to 375°F.

2. Place peppers and onions in large mixing bowl. Toss with olive oil and black pepper.

3. Spoon peppers and onions into large shallow baking dishes or onto cookie sheets with sides. Allow seasoned olive oil to remain in mixing bowl. Place peppers and onions in oven.

4. Meanwhile, stir zucchini and tomatoes into large mixing bowl with remaining seasoned olive oil.

5. After peppers and onions have roasted 10–12 minutes, add zucchini and tomatoes to baking dishes.

6. Roast 10–12 minutes, or until peppers are soft and vegetables have browned along the edges and wrinkled. Total roasting time will be 20–25 minutes.

7. Remove baking dishes from oven. Lift out peppers and place in bowl. Cover with plastic wrap. Let cool 10 minutes. Then peel and seed peppers over a bowl, saving the juices.

8. Coarsely chop all vegetables.

9. Place chopped vegetables in food processor together with garlic, basil, oregano, and 1 cup cold water.

10. Blend at high speed until smooth. Strain through a fine mesh sieve.

11. Place mixture in covered container. Refrigerate 4 hours before serving.

12. Adjust seasoning with pepper to taste.

13. Mix in lime juice just before serving.

Stuffed Sweet Pepper Soup

Moreen Weaver,
Bath, NY

Makes 10 servings
Prep. Time: 20 minutes
Cooking Time: 1 hour

1 lb. ground beef

2 qts. low-sodium tomato juice

3 medium red, or green, bell peppers, diced

1½ cups chili sauce, no salt added

1 cup uncooked brown rice

2 celery ribs, diced

1 large onion, diced

3 low-sodium chicken bouillon cubes

2 cloves garlic, minced

1. In large kettle over medium heat, cook beef until no longer pink. Drain off drippings.

2. Add remaining ingredients. Bring to a boil.

3. Reduce heat. Simmer, uncovered, for 1 hour, or until rice is tender.

Quickie French Onion Soup

**Mary Puskar,
Forest Hill, MD**

Makes 6-8 servings
Prep Time: 5-10 minutes
Cooking Time: 1 hour

½ stick (4 Tbsp.) butter

3-4 good-sized onions (enough to make 5 cups sliced onions)

¼ cup flour

6 cups beef broth, or 3 14½-oz. cans beef broth, or 6 cups water with 6 beef bouillon cubes

6-8 melba rounds, *optional*

2 cups grated mozzarella cheese, *optional*

1. Melt butter in a large saucepan.

2. Meanwhile, slice onions.

3. Sauté onions in butter. After they become tender, continue cooking over low heat so that they brown and deepen in flavor, up to 30 minutes.

4. Sprinkle with flour. Cook 2 minutes.

5. Stir in broth, or water and bouillon cubes. Cover.

6. Heat to boiling and simmer 20 minutes.

7. Ladle into individual ramekins or serving bowls (be sure they can withstand broiler heat).

8. Top each with melba rounds and/or grated cheese if you wish. Broil until cheese melts.

Creamy Asparagus Soup

Mary E. Riha,
Antigo, WI

Makes 4 servings
Prep. Time: 30 minutes
Cooking Time: 15–20 minutes

¼ cup sesame seeds

2 Tbsp. olive oil

1 medium onion, chopped

2 medium potatoes, cubed

4 cups chicken stock, *divided*

1 lb. raw asparagus, broken in 1-inch pieces

1 tsp. salt

dash of pepper

dash of nutmeg

sour cream

salted sunflower seeds, *optional*

1. In stockpot, sauté sesame seeds in olive oil until brown. Add onion and potatoes. Cook and stir until potatoes begin to stick.

2. Add 2 cups stock, asparagus, salt, and pepper. Bring to boil. Reduce heat and simmer until potatoes are done.

3. Carefully pour one fourth of hot mixture into blender. Cover and blend until smooth. (Hold the lid on with a potholder to keep the heat from pushing it off.)

4. Put pureed soup back in stockpot. Continue blending cooked soup, one-fourth at a time. Continue to add pureed soup back into stockpot.

5. When all soup has been pureed, add 2 more cups chicken stock to soup in stockpot. Heat thoroughly.

6. Add a dash of nutmeg.

7. Top each serving with a dollop of sour cream, and a sprinkling of sunflower seeds, if desired.

Cheesy Broccoli Cauliflower Soup

Marcia S. Myer, Manheim, PA

Makes 5–6 servings
Prep. Time: 20 minutes
Cooking Time: 40–45 minutes

6 Tbsp. butter

¼ cup chopped onion

½ cup flour

2 cups milk

1 cup (4 oz.) cubed Velveeta or American cheese

2 14-oz. cans chicken broth

2 cups chopped broccoli, fresh or frozen

2 cups chopped cauliflower, fresh or frozen

¼ cup finely chopped or grated carrots

¼ cup chopped celery

salt, to taste

¼ tsp. pepper

1. Melt butter in large saucepan. Stir in onion and sauté until just tender.

2. Stir in flour until well blended. Slowly add milk over medium heat, stirring constantly until thickened and smooth.

3. Stir in cheese, continuing to stir until cheese melts. Set aside.

4. In a separate saucepan, simmer broccoli, cauliflower, carrots, and celery in chicken broth until almost tender.

5. Season with salt, if you wish, and pepper.

6. Pour cheesy sauce into vegetables and heat through.

Creamy Broccoli Soup

**SuAnne Burkholder,
Millersburg, OH**

Makes 3–4 servings
Prep. Time: 10–15 minutes
Cooking Time: 15–20 minutes

4 cups milk, *divided*

1 Tbsp. chicken-flavored soup base

1½ cups cut-up broccoli

2 Tbsp. cornstarch

salt, to taste

1. Heat 3 cups milk and chicken base in a stockpot over low heat until hot.

2. Meanwhile, place cut-up broccoli in a microwave-safe dish. Add 1 Tbsp. water. Cover. Microwave on High for 1½ minutes. Stir. Repeat until broccoli becomes bright green and just-tender. Be careful not to overcook it! Drain broccoli of liquid.

3. In a small bowl, or in a jar with a tight-fitting lid, mix together 1 cup milk and cornstarch until smooth. Slowly add to hot milk mixture.

4. Simmer gently, stirring constantly. When slightly thickened, add broccoli and salt.

Egg Drop Soup

**Susan Guarneri,
Three Lakes, WI**

Makes 6-7 servings
Prep. Time: 10 minutes
Cooking Time: 25 minutes

2 Tbsp. cornstarch

6 cups chicken stock

2 Tbsp. soy sauce

3 Tbsp. white vinegar

1 small onion, minced

3 eggs, beaten

salt and pepper, to taste

sweet pepper flakes, *optional*

1. In stockpot, mix cornstarch with ½ cup cold chicken stock. When smooth, gradually add remaining chicken stock over medium heat, stirring continuously to keep cornstarch suspended and mixture smooth. Turn heat to low.

2. Add soy sauce, vinegar, and onion. Bring to low simmer (barely boiling).

3. Quickly stir in beaten eggs, swirling the broth and eggs in a circular motion to create "egg threads" in the soup. When all eggs are in the broth, allow to cook without stirring for 1 minute.

4. Remove pan from heat. Add salt and pepper to taste. Add sweet pepper flakes, if dcsired, before serving.

Garden Vegetable Soup with Pasta

**Jan McDowell,
New Holland, PA**

Makes 6 servings
Prep. Time: 20 minutes
Cooking Time: 30 minutes

1 Tbsp. olive oil

1 chopped onion

1 tsp. chopped garlic

1 small zucchini, chopped

½ lb. fresh mushrooms, sliced or chopped

1 bell pepper, chopped

24-oz. can chopped tomatoes, no salt added, undrained, or 10–12 whole tomatoes, peeled and chopped

1 Tbsp. fresh basil

2 cups water

3 reduced-sodium vegetable bouillon cubes

2 cups whole-grain rotini, cooked

dash of hot sauce, *optional*

1. Heat olive oil in 4-quart saucepan.

2. Sauté onion and garlic in oil until tender.

3. Add zucchini, mushrooms, bell pepper, tomatoes, basil, water, and bouillon.

4. Bring to a boil. Cover and simmer 10 minutes.

5. Meanwhile, cook rotini and drain. Add to soup.

6. Cover and heat through.

7. Pass hot sauce to be added to individual servings, if desired.

SLOW COOKER

Fresh Tomato Soup

**Rebecca Leichty,
Harrisonburg, VA**

Makes 6 servings
Prep. Time: 20–25 minutes
Cooking Time: 3–4 hours
Ideal slow-cooker size: 3½- or 4-qt.

5 cups diced ripe tomatoes (your choice whether
  or not to peel them)

1 Tbsp. tomato paste

4 cups salt-free chicken broth

1 carrot, peeled, grated

1 small onion, minced

1 Tbsp. fresh minced garlic

2 tsp. fresh chopped basil

pepper, to taste

2 Tbsp. fresh lemon juice

1 dried bay leaf

1. Combine all ingredients in a slow cooker.

2. Cook on Low for 3–4 hours. Stir once while
cooking.

3. Remove bay leaf before serving.

Tomato Basil Soup

Barbara Kuhns,
Millersburg, OH

Makes 4–6 servings
Prep. Time: 15 minutes
Cooking Time: 25 minutes

1 stick (8 Tbsp.) butter

¼ cup finely chopped onion

2 10½-oz. cans condensed tomato soup

2 cups tomato sauce

6-oz. can tomato paste

2 14½-oz. cans chicken broth

3 tsp. basil

¼ cup brown sugar

garlic cloves, minced, *optional*

⅓ cup flour

1 cup heavy whipping cream

1. Melt butter in soup pot.

2. Add and sauté onion until softened.

3. Add condensed soup, sauce, paste, broth, basil, brown sugar, and garlic (if using).

4. Cook, covered, until hot.

5. Whisk together flour and cream.

6. Add and heat gently, stirring, until soup is steaming and thick. Do not boil.

SLOW COOKER

Slow-Cooker Tomato Soup

**Becky Fixel,
Grosse Pointe Farms, MI**

Makes 8 servings
Prep. Time: 15 minutes
Cooking Time: 6 hours
Ideal slow-cooker size: 6-qt.

6–8 cups chopped fresh tomatoes

1 medium onion, chopped

2 tsp. fresh minced garlic

2 tsp. fresh chopped basil

½ tsp. pepper

½ tsp. sea salt

½ tsp. red pepper flakes

2 Tbsp. chicken bouillon

1 cup water

¾ cup half-and-half

1. Combine tomatoes, onion, spices, chicken bouillon, and 1 cup of water in your slow cooker.

2. Cover and cook on low for 6 hours.

3. Add in half-and-half and combine all ingredients with an immersion blender. Serve hot.

QUICK PREP

Flavorful Tomato Soup

Shari Ladd,
Hudson, MI

Makes 4 servings
Prep. Time: 10 minutes
Cooking Time: 20 minutes

2 Tbsp. chopped onions

1 Tbsp. extra-virgin olive oil

3 Tbsp. flour

2 tsp. sugar

½ tsp. pepper

¼ tsp. dried basil

½ tsp. dried oregano

¼ tsp. dried thyme

1 qt. stewed tomatoes, no salt added, undrained

2 cups milk

1. Sauté onions in oil in stockpot.

2. Stir in flour, sugar, and seasonings.

3. Stir in stewed tomatoes. Bring to a boil stirring constantly, and boil 1 minute.

4. Add 2 cups milk. If soup is too thick, add a little water. Stir well.

5. Simmer 10 minutes but do not boil.

Baked Potato Soup

**Flo Quint,
Quinter, KS
Susan Nafziger,
Canton, KS**

Makes 6-8 servings
Prep. Time: 30 minutes
Cooking Time: 15-20 minutes

1½ sticks (12 Tbsp.) butter

⅔ cup flour

7 cups milk

4 cups baked potatoes (about 5 large potatoes), peeled and cubed

4 green onions, sliced thin

8-12 strips bacon (according to your taste preference), cooked and crumbled

1¼ cups shredded cheese

8 oz. sour cream, *optional*

¾ tsp. salt, *optional*

¼ tsp. pepper, *optional*

1. Melt butter in large stockpot. Add flour and stir until smooth over medium heat.

2. Add milk, stirring often until thickened. Be careful not to scorch.

3. Add potatoes and onions and bring to a boil. Reduce heat and simmer 5 minutes, stirring often.

4. Remove from heat and add bacon, cheese, and sour cream if desired. Stir until melted.

5. Add seasonings if desired and blend thoroughly.

Vegetarian Split Pea Soup

**Colleen Heatwole,
Burton, MI**

Makes 6 servings
Prep. Time: 30 minutes
Cooking Time: 5–6 hours
Ideal slow-cooker size: 6-qt.

1 lb. split peas, sorted and rinsed

2 quarts gluten-free low-sodium vegetable broth

2 cups water

1 large onion, chopped

2 cloves garlic, minced

3 ribs celery, chopped

3 medium carrots, chopped finely

2 bay leaves

1 tsp. kosher salt

1 tsp. black pepper

1. Combine all ingredients and add to slow cooker.

2. Cover and cook on low 5–6 hours. Remove bay leaves and serve.

TIP

If creamy texture is desired, blend with immersion blender before serving.

SLOW COOKER

QUICK PREP

Spring Pea Soup

**Ary Bruno,
Stevenson, MD**

Makes 4-6 servings
Prep. Time: 15 minutes
Cooking Time: 4 hours
Ideal slow-cooker size: 4-qt.

2 cups fresh shelled peas

3 cups chicken stock

1 rib celery, minced

2 scallions, minced

1 Tbsp. fresh chopped mint, *divided*

pinch dried thyme

salt, to taste

1 cup milk, room temperature

2 Tbsp. flour

1. Place peas, stock, celery, scallions, ½ Tbsp. mint, and thyme in slow cooker. Add salt to taste.

2. Cover and cook on Low for 3 hours, until peas are tender.

3. Add remaining ½ Tbsp. mint.

4. Use immersion blender to puree soup.

5. Whisk together milk and flour. Whisk into soup and cook on High for 30–40 minutes, until thickened. Add salt to taste.

Carrot Ginger Soup

Jean Harris Robinson, Pemberton, NJ

Makes 8–10 servings
Prep. Time: 30 minutes
Cooking Time: 3¼–4¼ hours
Ideal slow-cooker size: 4-qt.

1 Tbsp. olive oil

3 lbs. carrots, peeled and thinly sliced

2 Tbsp. chopped ginger

2 Tbsp. minced scallion

3 ribs celery, chopped

49½-oz. can chicken broth

1 tsp. kosher salt

1 tsp. ground pepper

2 Tbsp. honey

1 cup half-and-half

1. Pour olive oil into slow cooker. Swirl to cover bottom of cooker.

2. Add carrots, ginger, scallion, and celery.

3. Pour in broth. Add salt, pepper, and honey. Stir to mix all ingredients well.

4. Cover. Cook on High 3–4 hours, or until carrots are soft.

5. Pulse with an immersion blender to purée.

6. Stir in half-and-half. Heat soup 15–20 minutes until heated through, but don't let it boil. Serve immediately.

Orange Soup

**Carolyn Spohn,
Shawnee, KS**

Makes 4-6 servings
Prep. Time: 15 minutes
Cooking Time: 3–4 hours
Ideal slow-cooker size: 4-qt.

4 cups chopped orange vegetables such as carrots, winter squash, red or orange bell pepper, sweet potato, etc.

4 cups broth of choice

1 small onion, chopped

1 tart apple, cored and chopped

date syrup or brown sugar, to taste

1. Place all ingredients in slow cooker.

2. Cover and cook until vegetables are soft, 3–4 hours on High.

3. Puree with immersion blender, or transfer soup to stand blender and puree with lid slightly ajar for steam to escape.

Potato-Cheese Soup

Mary Kathryn Yoder,
Harrisonville, MO

Makes 5 servings
Prep. Time: 20 minutes
Cooking Time: 20 minutes

4 medium-sized potatoes, peeled and cut into chunks

4 slices bacon

1 small onion, chopped, *optional*

4 cups milk

¾ tsp. salt

pepper, to taste

¾ cup shredded cheese, your choice of flavors

1. Place potato chunks in a saucepan. Add 1 inch water. Cover and cook over low heat until very tender.

2. Meanwhile, cut bacon into 1-inch lengths. Place in a large saucepan, along with the onion if you wish. Cook until tender.

3. When potatoes become tender, mash in their cooking water.

4. Add mashed potatoes and milk to bacon, and onion if using.

5. Stir in salt, pepper, and cheese. Cook over low heat, stirring occasionally to distribute cheese as it melts.

6. Soup is ready when cheese is melted and soup is hot.

TIPS

1. When you mash the potatoes, you can let them be a little lumpy. That adds interesting texture to the soup.
2. You can use leftover mashed potatoes to make this recipe if you have them.

Spinach and Potato Soup

Jane S. Lippincott,
Wynnewood, PA

Makes 9 servings
Prep. Time: 30 minutes
Cooking Time: 45–50 minutes

2 ribs celery, chopped

1 medium onion, chopped

1 clove garlic, minced

6 cups chopped fresh spinach

2 Tbsp. olive oil

4 potatoes, unpeeled and sliced ¼" thick

32 oz. chicken or vegetable stock, or less,
    depending upon how thick you like your soup

1 tsp. mustard seeds

1 Tbsp. white wine vinegar

pepper to taste

chopped chives for garnish

1. Chop celery, onion, garlic, and spinach first so they're ready. Set aside, keeping vegetables separate from each other.

2. In large stockpot heat olive oil on low or medium. Add onion. Cook until soft, about 10 minutes.

3. Add garlic and cook just until slightly softened.

4. Add celery, sliced potatoes, stock, and mustard seeds. Cover and simmer 25–30 minutes, or until potatoes are soft.

5. Use a potato masher to mash the mixture up a bit.

6. Add chopped spinach and vinegar. Simmer uncovered for 10 minutes more.

7. Serve with pepper and chives sprinkled on top of individual servings.

SLOW COOKER

QUICK PREP

Good Old Potato Soup

Jeanne Hertzog, Bethlehem, PA
Marcia S. Myer, Manheim, PA
Rhonda Lee Schmidt, Scranton, PA
Mitzi McGlynchey, Downingtown, PA
Vera Schmucker, Goshen, IN
Kaye Schnell, Falmouth, MA
Elizabeth Yoder, Millersburg, OH

Makes 8–10 servings
Prep. Time: 15 minutes
Cooking Time: 3–6 hours
Ideal slow-cooker size: 6-qt.

6 potatoes, peeled or not, and cubed

2 leeks, chopped

2 onions, chopped

1 rib celery, sliced

4 chicken bouillon cubes

5 cups water

1 Tbsp. salt

pepper to taste

5⅔ Tbsp. (⅓ cup) butter

13-oz. can evaporated milk

2 Tbsp. fresh chopped parsley

1. Grease interior of slow-cooker crock.

2. Combine all ingredients except milk and parsley in slow cooker.

3. Cover. Cook on Low 4–6 hours, or on High 3–4 hours.

4. Stir in milk during last hour.

5. Stir in parsley just before serving.

TIP

Mash the potatoes with an immersion blender or a potato masher for a thicker consistency soup.

SLOW COOKER

Simple Potato Soup

**Joyce Cox,
Port Angeles, WA**

Makes 6 servings
Prep. Time: 10 minutes
Cooking Time: 6 hours
Ideal slow-cooker size: 4-qt.

6 potatoes, peeled and diced

5 cups low-sodium vegetable broth

2 cups diced onions

½ cup diced celery

½ cup diced carrots

¼ tsp. ground pepper

1½ cups evaporated milk

3 Tbsp. chopped fresh parsley

1. Combine potatoes, broth, onions, celery, carrots, and pepper in slow cooker.

2. Cover and cook on Low for 6 hours or until vegetables are tender.

3. Stir in evaporated milk and parsley. Taste to correct seasonings. Allow to heat on Low an additional 30 minutes.

Hearty Lentil and Barley Soup

**Sherri Grindle,
Goshen, IN**

Makes 10 servings
Prep. Time: 15 minutes
Cooking Time: 65 minutes

2 ribs celery, thinly sliced

1 medium onion, chopped

1 clove garlic, minced

2 Tbsp. olive oil

6 cups water

28-oz. can diced tomatoes, no salt added, undrained, or 10–12 whole tomatoes, peeled and diced

¾ cup uncooked lentils, rinsed

¾ cup uncooked pearl barley

2 Tbsp. (or 3 cubes) low-sodium chicken bouillon granules

1½ tsp. fresh chopped oregano

1½ tsp. fresh chopped rosemary

¼ tsp. pepper

1 cup thinly sliced carrots

1 cup (4 oz.) shredded Swiss cheese, *optional*

1. In Dutch oven or soup kettle, sauté celery, onion, and garlic in oil until tender.

2. Add water, tomatoes, lentils, barley, bouillon, oregano, rosemary, and pepper.

3. Bring to a boil. Reduce heat, cover, and simmer 40 minutes, or until lentils and barley are almost tender.

4. Add carrots. Cover and simmer 15 minutes, or until carrots, lentils, and barley are tender.

5. If you wish, sprinkle each serving with 1 rounded Tbsp. cheese.

Lentil Soup

**Marcia S. Myer,
Manheim, PA**

Makes 6 servings
Prep. Time: 15 minutes
Cooking Time: 1 hour

2 large onions, chopped

1 carrot, chopped

½ tsp. dried thyme

½ tsp. dried marjoram

3 cups chicken or vegetable broth

1 cup uncooked lentils

¼ cup chopped fresh parsley

1 lb. canned tomatoes, no salt added, undrained

¼ cup sherry, *optional*

⅔ cup grated cheese, *optional*

1. Spray bottom of large stockpot with nonstick cooking spray. Sauté onions and carrot 3–5 minutes.

2. Add thyme and marjoram.

3. Add broth, lentils, parsley, and tomatoes.

4. Cover and simmer about 45 minutes, or until lentils are tender.

5. Stir in sherry if you wish.

6. Top each individual serving of soup with 1½ Tbsp. grated cheese if you wish.

Tomato and Barley Soup

Lizzie Ann Yoder,
Hartville, OH

Makes 6 servings
Prep. Time: 20–30 minutes
Cooking Time: 1–1½ hours

½ cup uncooked medium barley

1 cup chopped onion

2 ribs celery, including tops, cut up

3 cups chopped fresh tomatoes

2 Tbsp. fresh basil

6 cups chicken or vegetable stock

1–2 cups sliced fresh mushrooms, *optional*

1. In large stockpot combine all ingredients.

2. Bring to a boil and simmer, covered, 1 to 1½ hours, or until barley is tender.

3. If you wish, stir in mushrooms 30 minutes before end of cooking time.

Lentil, Spinach, and Rice Soup

Jean Harris Robinson,
Cinnaminson, NJ

Makes 10 servings
Prep. Time: 15 minutes
Cooking Time: 1¾ hours

1 large onion, diced

2 carrots, diced

1 celery rib, diced

3 Tbsp. extra-virgin olive oil

1 cup uncooked lentils

6 cups chicken or vegetable stock

4 cups water

1 cup diced tomatoes

¼ cup uncooked brown rice

1 bag (about 8 cups) fresh spinach, washed, dried, and chopped (with large stems removed)

1. In large stockpot over medium heat, sauté onion, carrots, and celery in oil for 10 minutes.

2. Add lentils and sauté another 5 minutes. Stir often.

3. Add stock and water. Cover and simmer 45 minutes. Stir occasionally.

4. Add tomatoes and brown rice.

5. Cover and simmer another 40 minutes.

6. Stir in chopped fresh spinach.

7. Cover and cook 5 minutes more.

Wild Rice Mushroom Soup

Kelly Amos,
Pittsboro, NC

Makes 4 servings
Prep. Time: 15–20 minutes
Cooking Time: 35 minutes

1 Tbsp. olive oil

half a white onion, chopped

¼ cup chopped celery

¼ cup chopped carrots

1½ cups sliced fresh white mushrooms

½ cup white wine

2½ cups chicken broth

1 cup half-and-half

2 Tbsp. flour

¾ tsp. fresh chopped thyme

black pepper

1 cup cooked wild rice

1. Put olive oil in stockpot and heat. Carefully add chopped onion, celery, and carrots. Cook until tender.

2. Add mushrooms, white wine, and chicken broth.

3. Cover and heat through.

4. In a bowl, blend half-and-half, flour, thyme, and pepper. Then stir in cooked wild rice.

5. Pour rice mixture into hot stockpot with vegetables.

6. Cook over medium heat. Stir continually until thickened and bubbly.

SLOW COOKER

Barley Cabbage Soup

**Betty K. Drescher,
Quakertown, PA**

Makes 8 servings
Prep. Time: 20 minutes
Cooking Time: 4–10 hours
Ideal slow-cooker size: 3½- or 4-qt.

¼ cup dry pearl barley

6 cups meat or vegetable broth

1 cup chopped onion

3–4 cups green cabbage, finely chopped

¼ cup fresh parsley, chopped

½ tsp. celery salt

½ tsp. salt

⅛ tsp. black pepper

1 Tbsp. minute tapioca

1. Combine all ingredients in slow cooker.

2. Cover. Cook on Low 8–10 hours or on High 4–5 hours.

Beans 'n' Greens Soup

Teri Sparks,
Glen Burnie, MD

Makes 10 servings
Prep. Time: 30 minutes
Cooking Time: 6–8 hours
Ideal slow-cooker size: 4- or 5-qt.

1 lb. dried 13-bean mix

5 cups gluten-free vegetable broth

¼ cup scallions, chopped

½ tsp. black pepper

¼ cup fresh chopped parsley

1 yellow onion, coarsely chopped

3 cloves garlic, chopped

1 Tbsp. olive oil

6 cups fresh kale, torn in 2-inch pieces

Greek yogurt or sour cream, *optional*

1. Rinse and place beans in 4-quart slow cooker.

2. Add broth, scallions, pepper, and parsley.

3. In skillet, sauté yellow onion and garlic in oil. Add to beans in slow cooker.

4. Pile kale on top of bean mixture and cover with lid (crock will be very full).

5. Cook on High for 1 hour. Greens will have wilted some, so stir to combine all ingredients. Replace lid. Cook on Low for 6–8 hours.

6. Top individual servings with dollops of Greek yogurt or sour cream if you wish.

Vegetarian Kielbasa Soup

Janie Steele,
Moore, OK

Makes 6–8 servings
Prep. Time: 20 minutes
Cooking Time: 5 hours
Ideal slow-cooker size: 4 qt.

1 lb. vegetarian kielbasa, sliced thin

8 cups vegetable broth

2 14-oz. cans cannellini beans with juice

1 onion, diced

1 bay leaf

1 Tbsp. fresh chopped thyme

¼ tsp. red pepper flakes

8 oz. rainbow rotini, uncooked

3 cloves garlic, minced

1 lb. chopped fresh spinach

salt and pepper, to taste

1. In skillet, brown kielbasa slices over high heat until some edges are brown.

2. Transfer kielbasa to slow cooker.

3. Add broth, beans, onion, bay leaf, thyme, and red pepper to slow cooker.

4. Cover and cook on Low for 4 hours.

5. Add rotini and garlic. Cook an additional hour on Low, or until pasta is as tender as you like it.

6. Stir in chopped spinach. Add salt and pepper to taste. Remove bay leaf.

Black Bean and Pumpkin Soup

Bev Beiler,
Gap, PA

Makes 4–6 servings
Prep. Time: 30 minutes
Cooking Time: 45 minutes

2 medium onions, chopped

½ cup minced shallots

4 cloves garlic, minced

4–5 tsp. ground cumin

1 tsp. salt

½ tsp. ground pepper

1 stick (½ cup) butter

3 15½-oz. cans black beans, drained

1 cup chopped tomatoes

4 cups beef broth

1½ cups cooked pumpkin

½ lb. cooked ham, diced

3 Tbsp. vinegar

1. In a large soup pot, sauté onions, shallots, garlic, cumin, salt, and pepper in butter until vegetables are tender.

2. Stir in beans, tomatoes, broth, and pumpkin.

3. Simmer 25 minutes, uncovered, stirring occasionally.

4. Add ham and vinegar. Simmer until heated through.

Stews

Hearty Beef Stew

**Hope Comerford,
Clinton Township, MI**

Makes 6–8 servings
Prep. Time: 30 minutes
Cooking Time: about 2 hours

1½ lbs. stew beef

1 Tbsp. olive oil

4–5 carrots, chopped

4 stalks celery, chopped

1 large onion, chopped

4 small- or medium-sized potatoes, diced

14½- oz. can diced tomatoes

6-oz. can tomato paste

7 cups beef stock

1 tsp. onion powder

1 tsp. salt

1 tsp. pepper

1 tsp. oregano

2 bay leaves

1. Lightly brown the stew beef in 1 Tbsp. olive oil in the bottom of a stew pot.

2. Add in the carrots, celery, and onion and cook until the onions are translucent.

3. Add in the potatoes, diced tomatoes, tomato paste, beef stock, onion powder, salt, pepper, oregano, and bay leaves. Stir well.

4. Bring to a boil.

5. Reduce to a simmer and cover. Cook for an additional 2 hours. Remove bay leaves before serving.

SLOW COOKER

Colorful Beef Stew

**Hope Comerford,
Clinton Township, MI**

Makes 6 servings
Prep. Time: 20 minutes
Cooking Time: 8–9 hours
Ideal slow-cooker size: 4-qt.

2 lbs. boneless beef chuck roast, trimmed of fat
and cut into ¾-inch pieces

1 large red onion, chopped

2 cups low-sodium beef broth

6-oz. can tomato paste

4 cloves garlic, minced

1 Tbsp. paprika

2 tsp. dried marjoram

½ tsp. black pepper

1 tsp. sea salt

1 red bell pepper, sliced

1 yellow bell pepper, sliced

1 orange bell pepper, sliced

1. Place all ingredients in the crock, except the sliced bell peppers, and stir.

2. Cover and cook on low for 8–9 hours. Stir in sliced bell peppers during the last 45 minutes of cooking time.

Cider Beef Stew

**Jean Turner,
Williams Lake, British Columbia**

Makes 8 servings
Prep. Time: 30 minutes
Cooking Time: 8 hours
Ideal slow-cooker size: 3-qt.

2 lbs. stew beef, cut into 1" cubes

6 Tbsp. flour, *divided*

2 tsp. salt

¼ tsp. pepper

¾ tsp. fresh chopped thyme

3 Tbsp. cooking oil

4 potatoes, peeled and quartered

4 carrots, quartered

2 onions, sliced

1 rib celery, sliced

1 apple, cored and chopped

2 cups apple cider or apple juice

1-2 Tbsp. vinegar

½ cup cold water

1. Stir together beef, 3 Tbsp. flour, salt, pepper, and thyme. Brown the beef in oil in a skillet Do in two batches if necessary to avoid crowding the meat.

2. Place vegetables and apple in slow cooker. Place browned meat cubes on top.

3. Pour apple cider and vinegar over top.

4. Cover and cook on Low for 8–10 hours.

5. Turn slow cooker to High. Blend cold water with remaining 3 Tbsp. flour. Stir into hot stew.

6. Cover and cook on High for 15 minutes or until thickened.

Chicken and Chili Stew

**Susan Kasting,
Jenks, OK**

Makes 4 servings
Prep. Time: 20 minutes
Cooking Time: 30 minutes

14½-oz. can chicken broth, *divided*

1 lb. boneless, skinless chicken breasts, cut into
   bite-sized pieces

4 cloves garlic, minced

1–2 jalapeño peppers, seeded and diced

1 Tbsp. cornstarch

1 medium red bell pepper, diced

1 medium carrot, sliced

15-oz. can corn, no salt added, drained

1 tsp. cumin

2 Tbsp. chopped cilantro

1. In good-sized stockpot, heat ¾ cup broth to boiling.

2. Add chicken to broth. Cook about 5 minutes, or until no longer pink.

3. Add garlic and jalapeño peppers. Cook 2 minutes.

4. In a bowl, stir cornstarch into remaining broth.

5. When smooth, add to chicken mixture. Cook, stirring, until thickened.

6. Stir in remaining ingredients.

7. Cover. Let simmer 20 minutes, stirring occasionally.

Lentil Barley Stew with Chicken

**Ilene Bontrager,
Arlington, KS**

Makes 4 servings
Prep. Time: 15 minutes
Cooking Time: 1–2 hours

⅓ cup uncooked lentils

⅓ cup uncooked green split peas

⅓ cup uncooked pearl barley

1 carrot, finely diced

half an onion, chopped

1 small rib celery, sliced thin

¼ tsp. pepper

1 qt. chicken or beef broth

1 cup chicken, cooked and diced

1. Rinse lentils, peas, and barley.

2. Place in 4–6-qt. stockpot. Add all remaining ingredients, except chicken.

3. Simmer, covered, 1–2 hours, or until lentils, peas, and barley are soft.

4. Stir in chicken. Cover and heat through.

Mushroom Stew

**Lauren Bailey,
Mechanicsburg, PA**

Makes 10 servings
Prep. Time: 20 minutes
Cooking Time: 30–35 minutes

5 Tbsp. butter, *divided*

1 Tbsp. oil

2 bay leaves

1 large onion, chopped

2 cloves minced garlic (use more if you wish)

2 Tbsp. flour

1 cup chicken broth

1 cup tomato juice, or fresh tomato puree

2 cups cut-up tomatoes, fresh or canned

1½ lbs. fresh mushrooms, chopped

1 tsp. dried thyme

salt and pepper, to taste

1½ cups red wine

1. In medium-sized saucepan melt 2 Tbsp. butter and oil. Add bay leaves and onion. Sauté until onions are golden. Stir in garlic and sauté one more minute.

2. Stir in flour and lower the heat. Cook several minutes on low, stirring constantly.

3. Add broth and tomato juice. Stir with whisk to remove all lumps. Add cut-up tomatoes.

4. In larger pot, sauté mushrooms in 3 Tbsp. butter. Add thyme over high heat. Add tomato mixture, salt, and pepper. Lower heat and simmer for 20 minutes.

5. Remove bay leaves. Add wine and stir for one minute.

SLOW COOKER

Zucchini Stew

**Colleen Heatwole,
Burton, MI**

Makes 6 servings
Prep. Time: 30 minutes
Cooking Time: 4–6 hours
Ideal slow-cooker size: 6-qt.

1 lb. Italian sausage, sliced

2 ribs of celery, diced

2 medium green bell peppers, diced

1 medium onion, chopped

2 28-oz. cans diced tomatoes, or 20–22 whole
tomatoes, peeled and diced

2 lbs. zucchini, cut into ½-inch slices

2 cloves garlic, minced

1 tsp. sugar

1 Tbsp. fresh chopped oregano

1 tsp. Italian seasoning

1 tsp. salt, *optional* (taste first)

6 Tbsp. grated Parmesan cheese

1. Brown sausage in hot skillet about 5–7 minutes. Drain and discard grease.

2. Mix celery, bell peppers, and onion into cooked sausage and cook and stir until they are softened, 10–12 minutes.

3. Combine remaining ingredients, except Parmesan cheese, and add to slow cooker.

4. Cook on Low 4–6 hours. Garnish each serving with 1 Tbsp. Parmesan cheese.

Speedy International Stew

Mabel Shirk,
Mount Crawford, VA

Makes 4 servings
Prep. Time: 5 minutes
Cooking Time: 5–10 minutes

2 14½-oz. cans stewed tomatoes (Italian, Mexican, or Cajun)

15-oz. can black beans, drained and rinsed

16-oz. can corn kernels, drained and rinsed

salt, to taste

1. Place all ingredients in a medium saucepan.

2. Cover and cook over medium heat for 5–10 minutes, stirring occasionally. Add salt to taste.

Pirate Stew

**Nancy Graves,
Manhattan, KS**

Makes 6 servings
Prep. Time: 20 minutes
Cooking Time: 6 hours
Ideal slow-cooker size: 4-qt.

¾ cup sliced onion

1 lb. ground beef

¼ cup uncooked, long-grain rice

3 cups diced raw potatoes

1 cup diced celery

2 cups canned kidney beans, drained

½ tsp. salt

⅛ tsp. pepper

¼ tsp. chili powder

¼ tsp. Worcestershire sauce

1 cup tomato sauce

½ cup water

1. Brown onion and ground beef in skillet. Drain.

2. Layer ingredients in slow cooker in order given.

3. Cover. Cook on Low 6 hours, or until potatoes and rice are cooked.

Easy Southern Brunswick Stew

**Barbara Sparks,
Glen Burnie, MD**

Makes 12 servings
Prep. Time: 20 minutes
Cooking Time: 7–9 hours
Ideal slow-cooker size: 4-qt.

2 lbs. pork butt, visible fat removed

15.25-oz. can white corn

1¼ cups ketchup

2 cups diced, cooked potatoes

10-oz. pkg. frozen peas

2 10¾-oz. cans reduced-sodium tomato soup

hot sauce, to taste, *optional*

1. Place pork in slow cooker.

2. Cover. Cook on Low 6–8 hours. Remove meat from bone and shred, removing and discarding all visible fat.

3. Combine all ingredients in slow cooker.

4. Cover. Bring to boil on High. Reduce heat to Low and simmer 30 minutes. Add hot sauce if you wish.

Chilis

 **SLOW COOKER**

Quick and Easy Chili

**Carolyn Spohn,
Shawnee, KS**

Makes 3–4 servings
Prep. Time: 10 minutes
Cooking Time: 25 minutes

½ lb. ground beef, or turkey, browned and drained

1 medium-sized onion, chopped

2 cloves garlic, minced

2 15-oz. cans chili-style beans with liquid

8-oz. can tomato sauce

1. Brown ground beef in a large skillet.

2. Drain, leaving about 1 tsp. drippings in pan. Sauté onion and garlic until softened.

3. Add beans, with liquid, and the tomato sauce. Bring to a slow boil.

4. Reduce heat to simmer and cook for 15 minutes.

5. Return meat to skillet. Heat together for 5 minutes.

Adirondack Three Alarm Chili

**Joanne Kennedy,
Plattsburgh, NY**

Makes 8 servings
Prep. Time: 25 minutes
Cooking Time: 3 hours

1¾ lbs. ground beef

3 medium onions, diced

4 cloves garlic, crushed

1 green pepper, chopped

28-oz. can crushed tomatoes

2 15½-oz. cans kidney beans, drained

16-oz. can no-added-salt tomato sauce

1 Tbsp. brown sugar

1 tsp. dried oregano

¼–1 tsp. crushed red pepper

3 Tbsp. chili powder

1 tsp. salt, *optional*

1. Brown ground beef in large soup pot.

2. Add and sauté onions, garlic, and green pepper.

3. Add the rest of ingredients. Simmer on low heat for 3 hours.

Chunky Beef Chili

**Ruth C. Hancock,
Earlsboro, OK**

Makes 4 servings
Prep. Time: 30 minutes
Cooking Time: 1¾–2¼ hours

2 Tbsp. vegetable oil, *divided*

1 lb. beef stew meat, cut into 1½-inch -hick pieces

1 medium onion, chopped

1 medium jalapeño pepper with seeds, minced,
   optional

½ tsp. salt

2 14½-oz. cans chili-seasoned diced tomatoes

1. Heat 1 Tbsp. oil in stockpot over medium heat until hot.

2. Brown half of beef in oil. Remove meat from pot and keep warm.

3. Repeat with remaining beef. Remove meat from pot and keep warm.

4. Add remaining 1 Tbsp. oil to stockpot, along with the onion, and the pepper if you wish.

5. Cook 5–8 minutes, or until vegetables are tender. Stir occasionally.

6. Return meat and juices to stockpot. Add salt and tomatoes.

7. Bring to a boil. Reduce heat. Cover tightly and simmer 1¾–2¼ hours, or until meat is tender but not dried out.

Beef and Black Bean Chili

Eileen B. Jarvis,
Saint Augustine, FL

Makes 8 servings
Prep. Time: 15 minutes
Cooking Time: 15–20 minutes

1 lb. ground beef

2 15-oz. cans no-salt-added black beans, rinsed and drained, *divided*

½ cup water

1 cup medium, or hot, chunky salsa

2 8-oz. cans no-salt-added tomato sauce

1 Tbsp. chili powder

sour cream, *optional*

cheddar cheese, grated, *optional*

1. Brown meat in large saucepan over medium-high heat. Drain off drippings.

2. While meat cooks, drain, rinse, and mash 1 can black beans.

3. Add mashed beans, second can of rinsed and drained beans, water, salsa, tomato sauce, and chili powder to saucepan. Stir well.

4. Cover. Cook over medium heat for 10 minutes. Stir occasionally.

5. If you wish, top individual servings with sour cream and/or reduced-fat cheese.

Spicy White Chili

**Gloria L. Lehman,
Singers Glen, VA
Lauren Bailey,
Mechanicsburg, PA**

Makes 6 servings
Prep. Time: 20–25 minutes
Cooking Time: 25 minutes

1½ Tbsp. oil

1 large onion, chopped

2 cloves garlic, minced

2 cups chopped cooked chicken

4-oz. can chopped mild green chilies

½–1 Tbsp. diced jalapeño pepper, *optional*

1½ tsp. ground cumin

1 tsp. dried oregano

10½-oz. can condensed chicken broth

10½-oz. can refilled with water

15-oz. can great northern beans

½ tsp. cayenne pepper, or to taste

salt, to taste

6 oz. shredded Monterey Jack cheese

½ cup sour cream

chopped green onions, *optional*

fresh cilantro, *optional*

1. In large stockpot, sauté onion and garlic in oil over medium heat.

2. Add chicken, chilies, jalapeño pepper (if you wish), cumin, oregano, chicken broth, water, and beans to stockpot and stir well. Bring to a boil, reduce heat, and simmer, covered, 10–15 minutes.

3. Just before serving, add cayenne pepper, salt, cheese, and sour cream. Heat just until cheese is melted, being careful not to let the soup boil.

4. Serve at once, garnished with chopped green onions and fresh cilantro if desired.

TIP

If you don't have cooked chicken, cut up 1½ lbs. skinless chicken breasts (about 1½ breasts) into 1-inch chunks. Follow Step 2 and proceed with the directions as given, being sure to simmer until the chicken is no longer pink.

Turkey Chili

Julette Rush,
Harrisonburg, VA

Makes 5 servings
Prep. Time: 15 minutes
Cooking Time: 30 minutes

½ lb. ground turkey breast

1 cup chopped onions

½ cup chopped green bell pepper

½ cup chopped red bell pepper

14½-oz. can diced tomatoes, no salt added, undrained

15-oz. can solid-pack pumpkin

15½-oz. can pinto beans, rinsed and drained

½ cup water

2 tsp. chili powder

½ tsp. garlic powder

¼ tsp. black pepper

¾ tsp. ground cumin

14½-oz. can chicken broth

1 cup shredded cheddar cheese

1. In large stockpot, sauté turkey, onions, and bell peppers until turkey is browned and vegetables are softened.

2. Mix in tomatoes, pumpkin, beans, water, seasonings, and broth. Reduce heat to low.

3. Cover and simmer 20 minutes. Stir occasionally.

4. Top individual servings with cheese.

Sausage Chili

**Norma I. Gehman,
Ephrata, PA**

Makes 4–6 servings
Prep. Time: 15 minutes
Cooking Time: 15 minutes

1 lb. loose sausage

¼ cup diced onion

2 Tbsp. flour

15½-oz. can chili beans in chili sauce

14½-oz. can diced tomatoes, undrained

1. Brown sausage in a large stockpot.

2. Add diced onion. Cook over medium heat until tender.

3. When onion is cooked, sprinkle 2 Tbsp. flour over mixture. Stir until flour is absorbed.

4. Add chili beans and diced tomatoes with juice. Mix well.

5. Simmer, covered, for 15 minutes.

TIPS

1. For more zip, use hot Italian sausage.
2. Crumble corn chips into the bottom of each serving bowl. Spoon chili over top of chips. Or crumble corn chips over top of each individual serving.
3. Grate your favorite cheese over top of each individual serving.
4. This recipe tastes even better when warmed up a day later.

SLOW COOKER

Beef and Sausage Chili

**Dorothea K. Ladd,
Ballston Lake, NY**

Makes 6–8 servings
Prep. Time: 15 minutes
Cooking Time: 4–5 hours
Ideal slow-cooker size: 6- or 7-qt.

1 lb. ground beef

1 lb. bulk pork sausage

1 Tbsp. oil, *optional*

1 large onion, chopped

1 large green pepper, chopped

2–3 ribs celery, chopped

2 15½-oz. cans kidney beans

29-oz. can tomato purée

6-oz. can tomato paste

2 cloves garlic, minced

2 Tbsp. chili powder

2 tsp. salt

1. Grease interior of slow-cooker crock.

2. If you have time, brown ground beef and sausage in skillet. Drain and place meats in crock. If you don't have time, place meats in crock and use a wooden spoon to break them into small clumps.

3. Combine all remaining ingredients in slow cooker.

4. Cover. Cook on Low 4–5 hours.

TIP

While it takes longer to brown the beef and sausage in a skillet before putting them into the slow cooker, the advantage is that it cooks off a lot of the meats' fat. When you drain off the drippings, you leave the fat behind and put far less into the crock, and therefore into your chili.

Chicken Three-Bean Chili

**Deb Kepiro,
Strasburg, PA**

Makes 8 servings
Prep. Time: 15 minutes
Cooking Time: 1 hour

1 large onion, chopped

2 Tbsp. oil

2 cups diced cooked chicken

15½-oz. can kidney beans, rinsed and drained

15½-oz. can pinto beans, rinsed and drained

15½-oz. can black beans, rinsed and drained

2 14½-oz. cans diced tomatoes

1 cup no-added-salt chicken broth

¾ cup salsa

1 tsp. cumin

shredded cheese, *optional*

green onions, *optional*

sour cream, *optional*

1. In a soup pot, sauté onion in oil until tender.

2. Add chicken, beans, tomatoes, broth, salsa, and cumin.

3. Bring to a boil. Reduce heat and let simmer for 30–60 minutes.

4. If desired, garnish with shredded cheese, green onions, and sour cream.

Chicken Barley Chili

**Colleen Heatwole,
Burton, MI**

Makes 10 servings
Prep. Time: 20 minutes
Cooking Time: 6–8 hours
Ideal slow-cooker size: 6-qt.

2 14½-oz. cans diced tomatoes

16-oz. jar salsa

1 cup quick-cooking barley, uncooked

3 cups water

14½-oz. can chicken broth

15½-oz. can black beans, rinsed and drained

3 cups cooked chicken, or turkey, cubed

15¼-oz. can whole-kernel corn, undrained

1–3 tsp. chili powder

1 tsp. ground cumin

sour cream, *optional*

shredded cheese, *optional*

1. Combine all ingredients except sour cream and cheese in slow cooker.

2. Cover. Cook on Low 6–8 hours, or until barley is tender.

3. Serve in individual soup bowls topped with sour cream and shredded cheese, if desired.

Vegetarian Chili

Lois Hess,
Lancaster, PA

Makes 8 servings
Prep. Time: 30 minutes
Cooking Time: 30 minutes

1 cup tomato juice, no salt added

½ cup raw bulgur

1 Tbsp. olive, canola, or saffron oil

4 cloves garlic

1½ cups chopped onion

1 cup chopped celery

1 cup chopped carrots

1 cup chopped tomatoes

1 tsp. cumin

1 tsp. dried basil

1–1½ tsp. chili powder, depending on your taste preference

1 cup chopped green bell peppers

2 16-oz. cans red kidney beans, rinsed and drained

juice of half a lemon

3 Tbsp. tomato paste, no salt added

dash cayenne pepper, or 1 tsp. coarsely ground black pepper

chopped fresh parsley, for garnish

1. Heat tomato juice to a boil. Pour over bulgur in a bowl. Cover and let stand 15 minutes.

2. Meanwhile, sauté garlic and onion in oil in large stockpot.

3. Add celery, carrots, tomatoes, and spices.

4. When vegetables are almost tender, add peppers. Cook until tender.

5. Stir in all remaining ingredients except parsley. Cover and heat gently.

6. Top individual servings with parsley.

White Bean Chili

Tracey Stenger,
Gretna, LA

Makes 12 servings
Prep. Time: 25 minutes
Cooking Time: 8–10 hours
Ideal slow-cooker size: 6-qt.

1 lb. ground beef, browned and drained

1 lb. ground turkey, browned and drained

3 bell peppers, chopped

2 onions, chopped

4 cloves garlic, minced

2 14½-oz. cans chicken or vegetable broth

15½-oz. can butter beans, rinsed and drained

15-oz. can black-eyed peas, rinsed and drained

15-oz. can garbanzo beans, rinsed and drained

15-oz. can navy beans, rinsed and drained

4-oz. can chopped green chilies

2 Tbsp. chili powder

3 tsp. ground cumin

2 tsp. dried oregano

2 tsp. paprika

½ tsp. salt

½ tsp. pepper

1. Combine all ingredients in slow cooker.

2. Cover. Cook on Low 8–10 hours.

Garden Chili

**Stacy Schmucker Stoltzfus,
Enola, PA**

Makes 10 servings
Prep. Time: 30 minutes
Cooking Time: 6–8 hours
Ideal slow-cooker size: 3½- or 4-qt.

¾ lb. onions, chopped

1 tsp. minced garlic

1 Tbsp. olive oil

¾ cup chopped celery

1 large carrot, peeled and thinly sliced

1 large green bell pepper, chopped

1 small zucchini, sliced

¼ lb. fresh mushrooms, sliced

1¼ cups water

14-oz. can kidney beans, drained

14-oz. can low-sodium diced tomatoes with juice,
  or 5–6 whole tomatoes, peeled and chopped

1 tsp. fresh lemon juice

½ tsp. fresh chopped oregano

1 tsp. ground cumin

1 tsp. chili powder

1 tsp. salt

1 tsp. black pepper

1. Sauté onions and garlic in olive oil in large skillet over medium heat until tender.

2. Add remaining fresh veggies. Sauté 2–3 minutes. Transfer to slow cooker.

3. Add remaining ingredients.

4. Cover. Cook on Low 6–8 hours.

No Beans Chili

**Sharon Timpe,
Jackson, WI**

Makes 10-12 servings
Prep. Time: 35 minutes
Cooking Time: Low 9-10 hours; High 6-7 hours
Ideal slow-cooker size: 5-6 qt.

¼ cup fresh chopped oregano

1 Tbsp. fresh chopped parsley

1 cup red wine

2-3 Tbsp. oil

1½ lbs round steak, cubed

1½ lbs. chuck steak, cubed

1 medium onion, chopped

1 cup chopped celery

1 cup chopped carrots

28-oz. can stewed tomatoes, or 10-12 whole
    tomatoes, peeled

8-oz. can tomato sauce

1 cup beef broth

1 Tbsp. vinegar

1 Tbsp. brown sugar

2 Tbsp. chili powder

1 tsp. cumin

¼ tsp. pepper

1 tsp. salt

1. Place oregano and parsley in red wine and set aside, ideally for about 15 minutes.

2. Heat oil in a skillet and brown the beef cubes. You may have to do this in two batches.

3. Put browned beef in slow cooker.

4. Add wine mixture to skillet and stir, scraping up browned bits. Scrape mixture into slow cooker.

5. Add rest of ingredients to slow cooker.

6. Cook on Low 9–10 hours or High 6–7 hours, until meat is very tender.

Chickpea Chili

**Thelma Wolgemuth,
Immokalee, FL**

Makes 8 servings
Prep. Time: 15 minutes
Cooking Time: 35–40 minutes

1 small onion, minced

2 cloves garlic, minced

15-oz. can garbanzo beans, drained

2 8-oz cans tomato sauce

1 Tbsp. chili powder

1 tsp. ground cumin

½ tsp. dried oregano

cayenne pepper, to taste

⅔ cup plain yogurt

2 cups hot cooked brown rice

1. Sauté onion and garlic over medium heat in a large saucepan.

2. Stir in garbanzo beans, tomato sauce, chili powder, cumin, oregano, and cayenne.

3. Simmer, uncovered, about 30 minutes, stirring occasionally. (If mixture becomes too thick, add water.)

4. Pour into serving dish and top with yogurt.

5. Serve with hot, cooked rice on the side.

QUICK PREP

SLOW COOKER

Summer Chili

Hope Comerford,
Clinton Township, MI

Makes 6 servings
Prep. Time: 15 minutes
Cooking Time: 3½–4 hours
Ideal slow-cooker size: 3-qt.

28-oz. can Red Gold sliced tomatoes and zucchini

15-oz. can tomato sauce

14-oz. can petite diced tomatoes with green chilies

15½-oz. can chili beans

15¼-oz. can black beans, drained and rinsed

1 medium onion, roughly chopped

3 small yellow squash, halved, quartered, and chopped

4 large cloves garlic, minced

¼ cup diced onion

1 tsp. salt

⅛ tsp. pepper

2 cups water

1. Place all ingredients into crock and stir.

2. Cover and cook on Low for 3½–4 hours.

Texican Chili

**Becky Oswald,
Broadway, VA**

Makes 15 servings
Prep. Time: 35 minutes
Cooking Time: 9–10 hours
Ideal slow-cooker size: 5- or 6-qt.

8 bacon strips, diced

2½ lbs. beef stewing meat, cubed

28-oz. can stewed tomatoes

14½-oz. can stewed tomatoes

8-oz. can tomato sauce

8-oz. can no-added-salt tomato sauce

16-oz. can kidney beans, rinsed and drained

2 cups sliced carrots

1 medium onion, chopped

1 cup chopped celery

½ cup chopped green pepper

¼ cup minced fresh parsley

1 Tbsp. chili powder

½ tsp. ground cumin

¼ tsp. pepper

1. Cook bacon in skillet until crisp. Drain on paper towel.

2. Brown beef in bacon drippings in skillet.

3. Combine all ingredients in slow cooker.

4. Cover. Cook on Low 9–10 hours, or until meat is tender. Stir occasionally.

Easy Chili

**Sheryl Shenk,
Harrisonburg, VA**

Makes 12 servings
Prep. Time: 20 minutes
Cooking Time: 3–8 hours
Ideal slow-cooker size: 5-qt.

1 lb. ground beef

1 onion, chopped

1 medium green pepper, chopped

½ tsp. salt

1 Tbsp. chili powder

2 tsp. Worcestershire sauce

29-oz. can no-added-salt tomato sauce

3 16-oz. cans kidney beans, drained

14½-oz. can crushed, or stewed, tomatoes

6-oz. can tomato paste

4 oz. grated cheddar cheese

1. Brown meat in skillet. Add onion and green pepper halfway through browning process. Drain. Pour into slow cooker.

2. Stir in remaining ingredients except cheese.

3. Cover. Cook on High 3 hours, or Low 7–8 hours.

4. Serve in bowls topped with cheddar cheese.

White Chili

Ruth E. Martin,
Loysville, PA

Makes 6 servings
Prep. Time: 15–20 minutes
Cooking Time: 20 minutes

2 cups diced potatoes, peeled or unpeeled

½ cup water

2 cups chopped broccoli, fresh, or 10-oz. pkg.
   chopped broccoli, frozen

2 Tbsp. onion

1 cup corn

¼–½ cup cooked, diced ham, *optional*

3 cups milk

½ tsp. salt, *optional*

⅛ tsp. pepper

1 tsp. powdered chicken bouillon, or 1 chicken
   bouillon cube

½ cup Velveeta cheese, cubed

1. In medium-sized saucepan, cook potatoes in water. When potatoes are almost soft, add broccoli and onion. Cook until tender.

2. Add corn, ham, if you wish, milk, seasonings, and bouillon. Heat, but do not boil.

3. Turn off and add cubed cheese. Let cheese melt for about 3–4 minutes. Stir and serve.

Chowders & Bisque

Basic Chowder Recipe

**Janie Steele,
Moore, OK**

Makes 6–8 servings
Prep. Time: 20 minutes
Cooking Time: 45 minutes

1 Tbsp. olive oil or butter

1–2 cups chopped onion

2 carrots, sliced

2 ribs celery, sliced

3–4 large potatoes, cubed

2 cups chicken broth

13-oz. can evaporated milk

½ tsp. garlic salt

pepper, to taste

2 cups milk

1. In oil or butter, sauté onion, carrots, and celery until they begin to soften.

2. Add potatoes and broth.

3. Bring to a boil, lower heat, and cover. Cook until potatoes soften.

4. Mash some of potatoes against side of pan.

5. Stir in evaporated milk, garlic salt, and pepper.

6. Add 2 cups milk.

7. Continue to cook and mash more potatoes until desired consistency.

Italian Clam Chowder

Susan Guarneri,
Three Lakes, WI

Makes 8 servings
Prep. Time: 30 minutes
Cooking Time: 4–5 hours

2 lbs. sweet Italian sausage

1 onion, chopped

4 medium potatoes, unpeeled and cubed

2 12-oz. cans beer

2 cups water or chicken broth

1 pt. cream

½ cup nonfat dry milk

1 dozen large fresh clams, chopped, or 6½-oz. can clams

8-oz. can minced clams

½ tsp. salt

¼ tsp. pepper

1 tsp. dried basil

1. Cut sausage into ½-inch slices. Place in large Dutch oven and brown until no longer pink. Set sausage aside.

2. Reserve 2 Tbsp. drippings in Dutch oven. Add onion, potatoes, beer, water or broth, cream, dry milk, clams, salt, pepper, and basil. Stir until well mixed.

3. Place Dutch oven in the oven. Bake at 275°F for 4–5 hours. (Do not increase the temperature or the chowder may boil and then the cream will curdle.)

4. One hour before the end of the baking time, stir in the reserved sausage.

Sweet Potato Chowder

**Deborah Heatwole,
Waynesboro, GA**

Makes 6 servings
Prep. Time: 15 minutes
Cooking Time: 25-30 minutes

1 celery rib, chopped

½ cup cooked, finely chopped, lean ham

2 Tbsp. olive oil

2 14½-oz. cans chicken broth

3 medium white potatoes, peeled and cubed

2 large sweet potatoes, peeled and cubed

2 Tbsp. dried minced onion

½ tsp. garlic powder

½ tsp. dried oregano

½ tsp. dried parsley

¼ tsp. black pepper

¼ tsp. crushed red pepper flakes

¼ cup flour

2 cups milk

1. In large stockpot, sauté celery and ham in oil.

2. Stir in broth. Add white and sweet potatoes and seasonings.

3. Bring almost to a boil. Reduce heat, cover, and simmer for 12 minutes, or until potatoes are tender.

4. Combine flour and milk in a bowl until smooth. Stir into soup.

5. Bring to a boil. Cook, stirring continually, for 2 minutes, or until thickened and bubbly. Be careful not to scorch or curdle milk.

Harvest Corn Chowder

Flossie Sultzaberger,
Mechanicsburg, PA

Makes 10 servings
Prep. Time: 20 minutes
Cooking Time: 40 minutes

1 medium onion, chopped

1 Tbsp. butter

2 14½-oz. cans no-salt-added cream-style corn

4 cups no-salt-added whole kernel corn

4 cups peeled, diced potatoes

6-oz. jar sliced mushrooms, drained

½ medium green pepper, chopped

½–1 medium sweet red pepper, chopped

10¾-oz. can lower-sodium, lower-fat mushroom soup

3 cups milk

pepper, to taste

½ lb. bacon, cooked and crumbled

1. In a large saucepan, sauté onion in butter until tender.

2. Add cream-style corn, kernel corn, potatoes, mushrooms, peppers, soup, and milk. Add pepper, to taste.

3. Simmer 30 minutes or until vegetables are tender.

4. To serve, garnish with bacon.

Salmon Chowder

Millie Martin,
Mount Joy, PA
Betty K. Drescher,
Quakertown, PA

Makes 6 servings
Prep. Time: 15-20 minutes
Cooking Time: 35 minutes

3 potatoes, diced

2 Tbsp. minced onion

2 Tbsp. diced celery

1 lb. can salmon, no salt added

½ cup corn

1 tsp. sage

1 tsp. dried basil

pepper, to taste

1 qt. milk

2 Tbsp. chopped fresh parsley

lemon zest, *optional*

1. In stockpot, cook potatoes, onions, and celery in small amount of water until tender.

2. Empty salmon into bowl. Remove bones and skin from salmon. Pull fish apart into pieces.

3. Add salmon, corn, sage, basil, pepper, and milk to vegetables in stockpot.

4. Cover. Heat slowly until very hot.

5. Top with chopped parsley, and lemon zest if you wish.

Broccoli Chowder

Ruth E. Martin,
Loysville, PA

Makes 6 servings
Prep. Time: 15–20 minutes
Cooking Time: 20 minutes

2 cups diced potatoes, peeled or unpeeled

2 cups water

2 cups chopped broccoli

2 Tbsp. diced onion

1 cup corn

¼–½ cup cooked, diced ham, *optional*

3 cups milk

½ tsp. salt, *optional*

⅛ tsp. pepper

1 tsp. powdered chicken bouillon, or 1 chicken
bouillon cube

½ cup Velveeta cheese, cubed

1. In medium-sized saucepan, cook potatoes in water. When potatoes are almost soft, add broccoli and onion. Cook until tender.

2. Add corn, ham, if you wish, milk, seasonings, and bouillon. Heat, but do not boil.

3. Turn off and add cubed cheese. Let cheese melt for about 3–4 minutes. Stir and serve.

Shrimp Chowder

Kristi See,
Weskan, KS
Karen Waggoner,
Joplin, MO

Makes 8 servings
Prep. Time: 20–25 minutes
Cooking Time: 3¼–4¼ hours
Ideal slow-cooker size: 5- or 6-qt.

1 lb. red potatoes, cubed

2½ cups chicken broth

3 celery ribs, chopped

8 scallions, chopped

½ cup chopped red bell peppers

1½ cups milk

1½ lbs. medium-sized shrimp, uncooked, peeled, and deveined

¼ cup all-purpose flour

½ cup evaporated milk

2 Tbsp. fresh minced parsley

½ tsp. paprika

½ tsp. Worcestershire sauce

⅛ tsp. cayenne pepper

⅛ tsp. black pepper

1. Combine potatoes, broth, celery, scallions, and red bell peppers in slow cooker.

2. Cover. Cook on Low 3–4 hours, or until vegetables are done to your liking.

3. Stir in 1½ cups milk and gently mash vegetables with potato masher. Leave some small chunks of potato.

4. Stir in shrimp.

5. Combine flour and evaporated milk. Mix until smooth. Gradually stir into soup mixture. Add remaining ingredients.

6. Cook and stir uncovered on high until thickened.

Ham and Potato Chowder

**Penny Blosser,
Beavercreek, OH**

Makes 5 servings
Prep. Time: 25 minutes
Cooking Time: 8 hours
Ideal slow-cooker size: 4-qt.

5-oz. pkg. scalloped potatoes

sauce mix from potato pkg.

1 cup cooked ham, cut into narrow strips

4 tsp. sodium-free bouillon powder

4 cups water

1 cup chopped celery

⅓ cup chopped onions

pepper, to taste

2 cups half-and-half

⅓ cup flour

1. Combine potatoes, sauce mix, ham, bouillon powder, water, celery, onions, and pepper in slow cooker.

2. Cover. Cook on Low 7 hours.

3. Combine half-and-half and flour. Gradually add to slow cooker, blending well.

4. Cover. Cook on Low up to 1 hour, stirring occasionally until thickened.

Corn and Shrimp Chowder

**Naomi E. Fast,
Hesston, KS**

Makes 6 servings
Prep. Time: 20 minutes
Cooking Time: 3–4 hours
Ideal slow-cooker size: 4- or 5-qt.

4 slices bacon, diced

1 cup chopped onions

2 cups diced, unpeeled red potatoes

2 10-oz. pkgs. frozen corn

1 tsp. Worcestershire sauce

½ tsp. paprika

½ tsp. salt

⅛ tsp. pepper

2 6-oz. cans shrimp

2 cups water

2 Tbsp. butter

12-oz. can evaporated milk

chopped chives

1. Fry bacon in skillet until lightly crisp. Add onions to drippings and sauté until transparent. Using slotted spoon, transfer bacon and onions to slow cooker.

2. Add remaining ingredients to cooker except milk and chives.

3. Cover. Cook on Low 3–4 hours, adding milk and chives 30 minutes before end of cooking time.

Manhattan Clam Chowder

**Joyce Slaymaker,
Strasburg, PA
Louise Stackhouse,
Benton, PA**

Makes 8 servings
Prep. Time: 25 minutes
Cooking Time: 8–10 hours
Ideal slow-cooker size: 4-qt.

¼ lb. bacon, diced and fried

1 large onion, chopped

2 carrots, thinly sliced

3 ribs celery, sliced

1 Tbsp. dried parsley flakes

28-oz. can chopped tomatoes

⅛ tsp. salt

2 8-oz. cans clams with liquid

2 whole peppercorns

1 bay leaf

1½ tsp. dried crushed thyme

3 medium potatoes, cubed

1. Combine all ingredients in slow cooker.

2. Cover. Cook on Low 8–10 hours.
Remove bay leaf and discard before serving.

Sausage and Kale Chowder

**Beverly Hummel,
Fleetwood, PA**

Makes 6 servings
Prep. Time: 20 minutes
Cooking Time: 5 hours
Ideal slow-cooker size: 4-5 qt.

1 lb. bulk sausage

1 cup chopped onion

6 small red potatoes, chopped

1 cup thinly sliced kale, ribs removed

6 cups chicken broth

1 cup milk, room temperature

salt and pepper to taste

1. Brown sausage. Drain off grease. Transfer sausage to slow cooker.

2. Add onion, potatoes, kale, and broth.

3. Cook on High for 4 hours, until potatoes and kale are soft.

4. Add milk and cook on Low for 1 hour. Season to taste with salt and pepper.

Tex-Mex Chicken Chowder

**Janie Steele,
Moore, OK**

Makes 8–10 servings
Prep. Time: 20 minutes
Cooking Time: 4½–6½ hours
Ideal slow-cooker size: 5-qt.

1 cup chopped onions

1 cup thinly sliced celery

2 cloves garlic, minced

1 Tbsp. oil

1½ lbs. boneless, skinless chicken breasts, cubed

32-oz. can chicken broth

1 pkg. country gravy mix

2 cups milk

16-oz. jar chunky salsa

32-oz. bag frozen hash brown potatoes

4½-oz. can chopped green chilies

8 oz. Velveeta cheese, cubed

1. Combine onions, celery, garlic, oil, chicken, and broth in 5-quart or larger slow cooker.

2. Cover. Cook on Low 2½ hours, until chicken is no longer pink.

3. In separate bowl, dissolve gravy mix in milk. Stir into chicken mixture. Add salsa, potatoes, chilies, and cheese and combine well. Cook on Low 2-4 hours, or until potatoes are fully cooked.

Crab Bisque

**Jere Zimmerman,
Reinholds, PA**

Makes 4 servings
Prep. Time: 15 minutes
Cooking Time: 20 minutes

1 stick (½ cup) butter, *divided*

½ cup finely chopped onion

½ cup finely chopped green pepper

2 scallions, finely chopped

¼ cup fresh chopped parsley

8 oz. fresh mushrooms, chopped

¼ cup flour

2 cups milk

1 tsp. salt

¼ tsp. pepper

3 cups half-and-half

16-oz. can (2½ cups) claw crabmeat

grated carrot for color, *optional*

1. Melt half a stick of butter in stockpot. Add onion, green pepper, scallions, parsley, and mushrooms. Cook until tender. Remove vegetables from heat and set aside.

2. In the same stockpot, melt remaining half stick of butter over low heat. Add flour and stir until smooth. Add milk, stirring until thickened.

3. Add reserved vegetable mixture, salt, pepper, half-and-half, crabmeat, and grated carrot, if desired.

4. Heat through over low heat, but do not boil.

Index

METRIC AND IMPERIAL CONVERSIONS

(These conversions are rounded for convenience)

Ingredient	Cups/Tablespoons/ Teaspoons	Ounces	Grams/Milliliters
Butter	1 cup=16 tablespoons= 2 sticks	7.5 ounces	209 grams
Cheese, shredded	1 cup	4 ounces	110 grams
Flour, all-purpose	1 cup/1 tablespoon	4.5 ounces/0.3 ounces	125 grams/8 grams
Fruits or veggies, chopped	1 cup	5 to 7 ounces	145 to 200 grams
Fruits or veggies, puréed	1 cup	8.5 ounces	245 grams
Herbs, dried	1 teaspoon	.05 ounces	1.5 grams
Lentils, uncooked	1 cup	7 ounces	200 grams
Liquids: cream, milk, water, or juice	1 cup	8 fluid ounces	240 milliliters
Salt	1 teaspoon	0.2 ounces	6 grams
Spices: cinnamon, cloves, ginger, or nutmeg (ground)	1 teaspoon	0.2 ounces	5 milliliters
Sugar, white	1 cup/1 tablespoon	7 ounces/0.5 ounces	200 grams/12.5 grams

Fahrenheit	Celcius	Gas Mark
225°	110°	¼
250°	120°	½
275°	140°	1
300°	150°	2
325°	160°	3
350°	180°	4
375°	190°	5
400°	200°	6
425°	220°	7
450°	230°	8